I0016238

A Modern Enterprise Architecture Approach

Transform the enterprise with Mobility, Cloud, IoT & Big Data

Dr Mehmet Yildiz
Distinguished Enterprise Architect

Revised Edition

October 2019

Revised Edition, September 2019

Copyright © Dr Mehmet Yildiz

Author contact: https://diigtalmehmet.com

Publisher: S.T.E.P.S. Publishing Australia

P.O Box 2097, Roxburgh Park, Victoria, 3064 Australia

info@stepsconsulting.com.au

Edited by Mark Longfield

Disclaimer

All rights reserved. No part of this publication may be produced, distributed, or transmitted in any form or by any means, including photocopying, printing, recording or other electronic or mechanical methods, without the prior written permission of the publisher. All other trademarks or registered trademarks are the property of their respective owners. This book is provided for information purposes only. Although the publisher, author, and editors have made every effort to ensure that the information in this book was accurate and correct during the publishing process, the publisher, author and editors do not assume and hereby disclaim any liability to any party for any loss, damage, or disruption caused by errors or omissions; whether such errors or omissions result from negligence, accident, or any other causes. Use of the information, instructions, and guidance contained in this book is at readers own risk.

Table of Contents

Chapter 1: Introduction

Purpose of this book

I authored this book to provide essential guidance, compelling ideas, and unique ways to Enterprise Architects so that they can successfully perform complex enterprise modernisation initiatives transforming from chaos to coherence. This is not an ordinary theory book describing Enterprise Architecture in detail. There are myriad of books on the market and in libraries discussing details of enterprise architecture. My aim here is to highlight success factors and reflect lessons learnt.

As a practising Senior Enterprise Architect, myself, I read hundreds of those books and articles to learn different views. They have been valuable to me to establish my foundations in the earlier phase of my profession. However, what is missing now is a concise guidance book showing Enterprise Architects the novel approaches, insights from the real-life experience and experimentations, and pointing out the differentiating technologies for enterprise modernisation. If only there were such a guide when I started engaging in modernisation and transformation programs.

The biggest lesson learned is the business outcome of the enterprise modernisation. What genuinely matters for business is the return on investment of the enterprise architecture and its monetising capabilities. The rest is the theory because nowadays sponsoring executives, due to economic climate, have no interest, attention, or tolerance for non-profitable ventures. I am sorry for disappointing some idealistic Enterprise Architects, but with due respect, it is the reality, and we cannot change it. This book deals with reality rather than theoretical perfection. Anyone against this view on this climate must be coming from another planet.

In this concise, uncluttered and easy-to-read book, I attempt to show the significant pain points and valuable considerations for enterprise modernisation using a structured approach. The architectural rigour is still essential. We cannot compromise the rigour aiming to the quality of products and services as a target outcome. However, there must be a delicate balance among architectural rigour, business value, and speed to market. I applied this pragmatic approach to multiple substantial transformation initiatives and complex modernisations programs. The key point is using an incrementally progressing iterative approach to every aspect of modernisation initiatives, including people, processes, tools, and technologies as a whole.

Starting with a high-level view of enterprise architecture to set the context, I provided a dozen of distinct chapters to point out and elaborate on the factors which can make a real difference in dealing with complexity and producing excellent modernisation initiatives. As eminent leaders, Enterprise Architects are the critical talents who can undertake this massive mission using their people and technology skills, in addition to many critical attributes such as calm and composed approach. They are architects, not firefighters. I have full confidence that this book can provide valuable insights and aha moments for these talented architects to tackle this enormous mission turning chaos to coherence.

Audience

This book can be an ideal source for Enterprise Architects who engage in enormous enterprise modernisation initiatives as the first time. The guidance in this book can jump-start the process. Another target audience type could be architects who are planning to be Enterprise Architects and to undertake transformation and modernisation initiatives in complex environments and large organisations.

In addition to architects, this book can provide useful insights to IT executives - CTO (Chief Technology Officer), CDO (Chief Digital Officer), CIO (Chief Information Officer), and Head of Enterprise Technologies - who are responsible for substantial enterprise modernisation and digital transformation programs.

From an execution perspective, this book can be also helpful for the program and portfolio managers responsible for enterprise modernisation programs.

As an educative resource, this book can also be useful for students studying Enterprise Architecture and relevant disciplines who want to understand the practical aspect of the discipline, especially from the modernisation and transformation perspectives.

Lessons Learned from my Background

I have been practising enterprise architecture over two decades. Large organisations are substantially challenged with rapid change in technology and increasing demands of consumers. Every large organisation that I worked for had some transformation and modernisation programs to some extent at the enterprise level. I witnessed several failed initiatives caused by multiple factors which could be in their control or beyond their control. One of the major causes of the failure was difficulty in dealing with complexity. Enterprises have multiple dimensions spanning to many domains. These domains are tightly interrelated; hence, a minor issue with one domain can be reflected in many others.

For example, in a typical large organisation, just strategy and planning phase took over a year while hundreds of highly paid employees were churning and debating the ideas extensively. Once the program finally reached a consensus on the scope and approached the requirements management phase, the entire budget for the program was consumed. The organisation had to make all those talented people redundant. This typical and unfortunate example was a valuable lesson learned on how important to approach the modernisation iteratively rather than trying to perfect everything upfront. From hindsight, they could have set the strategy at a high level for a single domain and only plan one aspect of the strategy in the selected domain, test it with the allocated budget, and produced some desirable results.

The other reasons for failure are too much focus on technologies which were challenging to implement at enterprise-wide due to inhibitive cost, lack of required functionality, and capabilities perspectives. For example, while an organisation could have started testing the Cloud with a cheap public Cloud offering and move their workloads iteratively, they were trying to build a full-fledged private Cloud platform with many emerging technologies and expensive gear. The hidden cost in such a monolithic approach, unfortunately, destroyed all good intentions.

There are many more similar lessons learned from failure; therefore, I want to share my experience how these deadly errors can be prevented with a different mindset, novel approach, an innovative structure, and with use of supportive tools, and empowering technologies.

Chapter 2: Fundamentals of Enterprise Architecture

Purpose

In this chapter, we cover the fundamentals of enterprise architecture briefly so that we all think on the same page. In any business venture, principally, fundamentals must be met first so that further progress goes on. For this reason, we start with the definition of enterprise architecture within the modernisation context and introduce the fundamental techniques to deal with enterprise complexity.

In consecutive chapters, as another fundamental aspect, we touch on the changing and essential roles and responsibilities of Enterprise Architects for leading successful modernisation initiatives. After setting these fundamentals, we high light other necessary pillars in this novel framework. Now, let's attempt to define enterprise architecture.

Defining Enterprise Architecture

The Enterprise Architecture (EA) discipline in Information Technology (IT) that defines a macro level IT architecture at the enterprise level focusing on the mapping of IT capabilities to business needs using a governance method. Traditionally, thought leaders used the town planning metaphor to define and visualise EA. So far, this town planning metaphor is the most prominent explanation to provide a common understanding of EA. Therefore, now and then in this book, we use this metaphor to convey the message and clarify the abstract points.

The focus of EA has been defining and describing the relationships, logical flows, implementation of business processes, activities, functions, data, information, applications, underlying technology, and supportive tools in the enterprise.

Vision, process and planning are the critical aspects of EA. These three aspects – vision, process, and planning- are driven by and closely aligned with business needs, capability, and requirements at the enterprise level.

EA has five distinct phases. The phases in order of maturity are initial, baseline, target, integrated, and optimised. Enterprise modernisation initiatives must consider these phases and deal with them both individually and in an integrated manner.

EA has several reference models to explain its fundamental domains. The most common models are BRM (Business Reference Model), CRM (The Components Reference Model), TRM (The Technical Reference Model), DMR (The Data Reference Model), PRM (Performance Reference Model). These models cover business capability, business functionality, technology standards, IT systems, data descriptions, and quality measurements. These models are well-established. For example, one of the most common EA methods, FEA (Federal Enterprise Architecture), also uses these models.

There are many traditional methods for Enterprise Architecture. The popular ones are TOGAF, Zachman, and FEA. Some large organisations have their established proprietary methodologies which are used for internal purposes and not shared publicly. However, knowing an established method and understanding the principles of enterprise architecture in a broad sense, Enterprise Architects can quickly learn other proprietary methods by reviewing them and working with the actual work products in a relatively short time.

Managing Enterprise Complexity

Enterprise environments can be extremely complex with multiple layers of systems, technologies, tools and processes. One of the critical roles of Enterprise Architects is to manage complexity. There are different approaches and techniques to manage complexity in enterprises.

The most common simplification technique is the partitioning approach. Some Enterprise Architects may use different terms for partitioning such as dividing, subdividing, segregating, and apportioning. These alternative terms all mean the same thing. The process of partitioning refers to making smaller parts of a large object. Let's say that we are dealing with a network system. We partition the overall network to smaller groups such as a wide-area network or a local-area network. We can partition the wide-area network from tools perspectives such as routers, switches and other devices.

Once we partition an overarching system, then we can start simplifying it to deal with complexity. Simplification is a broad technique. We can customise the process of simplification for different systems and activities. One way of simplifying a system is reducing the quantity. Take the number of servers, for example, looking at a thousand units of servers, and ten servers can make a massive difference. Another technique could be moving an item from a large group of the clustered items but still, keep the relationship to keep its core identity. This book offers a chapter on the importance of simplification for enterprise modernisation as it is a critical factor.

After partitioning and simplifying the third critical method is iterating. Probably you heard a lot about this term while working with agile methods. Iteration is progressing activities in smaller steps and chunks. Iteration is one of the best approaches to deal with complexity and uncertainty. Moving with iterative steps, we achieve some results. If the result is positive, we make progress and go to the next iteration. If the result is negative, we fail but learn how not to do it and try another iteration. The positive side of this negative result is that we fail cheap, and we fail quickly. Failing cheap and quickly don't make a big difference from a financial and project schedule perspective. As iteration is so critical in enterprise modernisation, this book offers a chapter on Agile methods and approach for successful modernisation initiatives.

In summary, we can remember these three basic methods using daily examples such as we have separate teams for different functions at work; this is partitioning of teams. We only belong to a single nation; this is a simplification. We plan for a school or certification exam chapter by chapter; this is iteration. There are also different tools that we use for these techniques. In various chapters of this book, we will cover them.

Enterprise Solutions Cost

Everything in enterprise transformation generates substantial cost. There are known and hidden costs. It is relatively more comfortable to deal with the known costs; however, the challenge is to deal with the hidden costs. Hidden costs are the more substantial part of the iceberg. Even though the cost is managed by financial teams, Enterprise Architects need to find ways to make enterprise modernisation solutions inexpensive, affordable and lowering the cost gradually without compromising quality. Quality considerations are the critical requirements of enterprise modernisation initiatives.

There is a common perception that making solutions cost-effective without compromising quality is not possible as a considerable number of trade-offs are made in the architecture development phase. It is true that there are many challenges and factors to be considered to achieve this goal.

However, the solution cost can be reduced by making trade-offs with a methodical approach by obtaining collaborative input from business and technology departments. We can also use the Agile approach appropriately. It is possible to increase the quality of the solutions by applying professional diligence, architectural rigour, delivery agility, and smart collaboration. These principle-based approaches are critical to maintain and increase quality.

Enterprise Architects need to participate in cost model development proactively. For example, we must develop a solution Bill of Materials (BOM) once we set the solution strategy and complete all high-level design artefacts. The BOM may include hardware, software, other procurement, and services costs.

Beware that there may be tremendous pressure from project managers and procurement staff to generate an upfront BOM to meet the project deadlines. No one wants to get blamed for any delay; hence there may be a huge rush to get things in place quickly. However, we can point out that without an approved architecture, no BOM can be formalised and released. This assertive and straightforward input from the Enterprise Architects can save a considerable amount of funds to the enterprise modernisation programs or save wasting well controlled and tight budgets.

There are extensive infrastructure and maintenance costs in the enterprise associated with large data centres, server farms, Mobile BI, Big Data, and hybrid clouds. These foundational infrastructure components can make enterprise solutions more viable from a cost perspective. However, a single failure or defect in a device or a group of devices serving the consumers can affect the service levels hence could lead to high costs for the service providers.

Availability and performance of the systems are the significant factors for punitive service levels. Automated SLAs can detect low availability and poor performance. These automated SLAs trigger the rules and force the organisations breaching the agreements pay the contractually agreed penalties. The downtime is the most critical factor for generating excessive penalties. The longer the systems are down, the higher the penalties.

Service downtime costs can be very high based on agreed rates and cause excessive penalties when accumulated for service-level breaches by organisations. Service Level breaches also have a strategic adverse effect on an organisation's product and services. For example, downtimes in services or defects in products can result in poor client satisfaction. If we also look at from the consumer perspectives, they lose business due to service downtimes. It is a lose-lose scenario even though the consumer organisations are compensated with SLA penalties paid by the service providers.

Enterprise Architects, we need to pay attention to the SLAs from the early stages of the modernisation solution life cycle. The higher the quality of the solutions, the easier it is for SLAs to meet when the solutions are in production and the operational state. The rigour for quality in each phase can positively contribute to deal with SLA risks.

Some of the key considerations to address SLA issues could be autonomous condition monitoring and remote maintenance. There are specialist solutions regarding these trending techniques. It can be useful to engage automation specialists for the design of these unique features in our modernisation solutions.

Service level management is also crucial in enterprise modernisation initiatives as one of the biggest fears of the business executives is if performance and availability problems damage their organisations' client satisfaction and compromising business revenues. To address the risks associated with this valid business fear, Enterprise Architects need to pay special attention to SLA strategy, planning, design and implementation in an integrated way.

Chapter Summary and Key Points

The Enterprise Architecture (EA) discipline in Information Technology (IT) that defines a macro level IT architecture at the enterprise level focusing on the mapping of IT capabilities to business needs using a governance method.

The focus of EA has been defining and describing the relationships, logical flows, implementation of business processes, activities, functions, data, information, applications, underlying technology, and supportive tools in the enterprise.

EA has five distinct phases. The phases in order of maturity are initial, baseline, target, integrated, and optimised. Enterprise modernisation initiatives must consider these phases and deal with them both individually and in an integrated manner.

The most common models are BRM (Business Reference Model), CRM (The Components Reference Model), TRM (The Technical Reference Model), DMR (The Data Reference Model), PRM (Performance Reference Model).

The most common simplification technique is the partitioning approach. Another way of simplifying a system is reducing the quantity. After partitioning and simplifying the third critical method is iterating.

Everything in enterprise transformation generates

substantial cost. There are known and hidden costs. It is relatively more comfortable to deal with the known costs however the challenge is to deal with the hidden costs.

Enterprise Architects need to pay attention to the SLAs from the early stages of the modernisation solution life cycle. The higher the quality of the solutions, the easier it is for SLAs to meet when the solutions are in production and the operational state.

Chapter 3: An Over of Enterprise Modernisation

Purpose

The purpose of this section is to provide high-level guidance on the steps to be taken in the enterprise modernisation programs which could serve as a generic checklist. These steps are based on some of my recent projects which posed substantial challenges from multiple angles; therefore, I attempt to highlight the problem areas so that you can consider them for your potential initiatives similar to mine. Assuming you are an experienced Enterprise Architect, I don't delve into how to perform general architectural tasks but focus on the critical items that really make a real difference for success.

Modernisation Scope

Enterprise modernisation is a long journey moving the enterprise from chaos to coherence. The modernisation process includes every aspect of the enterprise. Modernisation scope can be massive if we don't apply architectural discipline to it.

Business stakeholders can be very ambitious and ask many functions and features or modernise too many things in a single move with their good intentions. However, their intention may not match reality. As Enterprise Architects, we need to reflect the reality using some estimates for resourcing and timelines leveraging the skills of project, program and financial managers.

After understanding the scope of enterprise modernisation and have an idea about the predictive cost, we need to define the modernisation scope using architectural principles and guidelines. There may be a various aspect of the modernisation; hence in this book, we focus on the enterprise IT systems. Even though enterprise IT systems look only a tiny bit of an organisation in overarching enterprise, this domain by itself can be gigantic especially for the large organisations.

Enterprise IT systems include business IT processes, business data, business applications, IT infrastructure, and IT service delivery. These domains can even be more complicated with the addition of geographical factors such as adding multiple countries to the equation. The good news is that these primary domains can be modernised iteratively in parallel.

Both a top-down and bottom-up approach can be applied. At the top tier business, IT processes and at the bottom tier IT infrastructure. These two domains can independently be modernised using parallel activities. However, an integrated approach is essential as there can always be dependencies from multiple angles.

Depending on the organisation's size and complexity, the modernisation scope can be enormous. To give you some guidance, some of the modernisation programs I worked included Workplace, Hosting, Network, Communications, Business Applications, Infrastructure Tools, Workloads, Middleware, Web Services, Databases, Data Platforms, Helpdesk, and Legacy Backend. When you join these initiatives, it can be a mammoth program. Therefore, in the scope formulation phase, we need to be realistic by removing any emotions and set the expectations based on measurable estimates.

Once the modernisation scope and strategy is set by the team, Enterprise Architects refine the strategy and convert it to the architectural speak. The scope document usually refined by the program managers.

Modernisation Strategy

From an architectural point of view, the strategy document is a critical artefact to bring all parties and stakeholders on the same page. In our strategy, we need to identify the critical dependencies among multiple domains in the approved scope based on the short term, midterm and long-term considerations.

The solution strategy process provides an objective assessment of the current situation. It aligns the program goals with the organisational goals at the enterprise level and ensures that all gaps are covered. The solution strategy document also documents the opportunities, threats, strengths and weaknesses of the project from the technical, commercial and financial angles.

We know that the strategy of solutions hardly changes in the later phases of the solution process. Therefore, it must be understood and approved at earlier phases. However, we can make our strategy flexible by creating changeable tactics to empower our solution strategy. These tactics can also be documented and approved as part of the solution architecture approval process.

By using the strategy and considering the dependencies, we develop a high-level roadmap to inform the sponsoring executives.

Modernisation Roadmap

Modernisation roadmap can include the current state at a high level, the future state, primary transformational goals, and indicate the key outcomes, timelines and a ballpark cost for the overall modernisation. These indications can be very high level as there may be many factors affecting timelines and cost.

Once the roadmap for the enterprise modernisation is set the Enterprise Architects need to make a comprehensive viability assessment considering the current state of the scoped initiatives, their indicative future state and the strategies to reach the end state. The Viability Assessment helps the roadmap to be validated by technical leaders and approved by sponsoring executives.

Modernisation Viability Assessment

Enterprise modernisation viability assessment must include key risks, constraints, and dependencies at the enterprise level. These items need to be organised adequately to make sense for the executive stakeholders. For example, it should include the rating of risks with likelihood, implications and impact.

Dependencies need to be articulated using various clarifying points such as internal, external, financial, commercial and others. It is also necessary to define dependencies in an integrated manner, while there may also be some interdependencies between multiple components or building blocks in the roadmap. The type of dependency and the potential impact needs to be articulated in a centralised Viability Assessment work-product.

Each solution or domain architects develop their assessments however the enterprise architecture viability assessment is the most informative tool an Enterprise Architect can provide to the sponsoring executives to make informed decisions for the strategy and roadmap. Therefore, this work product needs to be prepared with architectural, technical, commercial, and financial rigour.

Modernisation Requirements

After review and approval of the viability assessment, we need to delve into collecting the high-level requirements of the solutions based on the domains that we mentioned earlier.

Dealing with the massive requirements of those domains can be daunting; therefore, as Enterprise Architects, we can delegate the requirements collection process with the domain and program architects including business analysts.

In this phase, the role of Enterprise Architect is to coordinate and facilitate the requirements management team which can consist of multiple architects and business analysts. This coordination and facilitation activities can be almost a full-time role. To this end, we need to use appropriate requirements management tools and systems available in our organisation.

I noticed that some organisation don't have such tools, and they use a simple spreadsheet to manage requirements. In this case, we need to find ways to automate the spreadsheet and keep it in a central repository allowing multiple authors to enter and manipulate data consecutively. In some smaller organisations recently, we used the Box to keep the requirements matrix in a shareable spreadsheet.

After requirements are collected and analysed at a reasonable amount, the next important activity is to prioritise the requirements based on business impact. Enterprise Architects need to develop criteria to prioritise the requirements based on factors depicted in the strategy and roadmap documents, as well as the financial and business priorities set by the sponsoring executives.

Once the requirements are prioritised, each requirement needs to be validated by the relevant users, sponsors and other associated stakeholders. The requirements validation process may take a considerable amount of time, based on the number of requirements. Some requirements can be comprehensive and may be difficult to validate easily. Therefore, it can be useful to sort these requirements into smaller groups.

As an architectural principle, requirements must be SMART — an acronym we use to describe the quality of requirements. Using the SMART acronym, we can confirm that the requirements must be specific, measurable, actionable, realistic and traceable.

One crucial aspect to the requirements analyses is the use of the MoSCoW rule, as adopted from the following Agile methods: 1) must have requirements; 2) should have, if at all possible; 3) could have, but not critical; 4) will not have this time, but potentially later.

Once the domain requirements from multiple domains are validated as mandatory, optional or unnecessary, the lead architects in each domain draft their solutions and commence the requirements' traceability activities across the modernisation solution building blocks, project or initiative.

Requirements traceability is a fundamental architectural activity that mandates rigour and governance. Requirements traceability has a considerable impact on the solution end product and services. If we fail to track the requirements to the solution building blocks, it can be challenging to meet the required service levels, and most likely, problems can arise in the project.

As Enterprise Architects, we guide the domain lead architects to pay utmost attention to both the functional and non-functional aspects of solutions. To this end, they start with requirements. Typically, we can categorise requirements under two main types: Functional and Non-Functional. Both functional and non-functional components apply to the enterprise modernisation programs. Coupled with the non-functional aspects, architectural rigour and flexibility need to be balanced to achieve functionality.

The lead domain and solution architects need to understand the details of both the functional and non-functional aspect of the solution well. Functional and Non-Functional requirements are like inseparable yin and yang. They need to be analysed and documented in an integrated manner. Let's briefly define these two types of requirements and understand their nature.

The functional requirements of a solution involve what the system offers to the consumers as functionality to be accomplished. For example, the system may offer calculations, data processing, and workflows. Functional requirements are usually related to the consumers of the solution. They describe what the consumers expect from the solution product and services.

Non-functional aspects involve how the system can accomplish these functionalities, such as performance, availability, security, reliability, scalability, usability, configuration, and so on. These are primarily technical and operational requirements. The tasks involved in the Non-Functional requirements relate to the IT support and maintenance teams.

Due to the multiple challenges surrounding the enterprise modernisation programs, developing a successful solution is not an easy task for any domain or solution architect. Requirements phase poses multiple architectural challenges. Some of these challenges related to the non-functional aspects are mobility, reliability, scalability, configuration management, availability, interoperability, security, and privacy.

Let's take scalability as an example. Enterprise modernisation solutions require overall scalability and comprehensive capacity plans. Multiple applications require integration with a myriad of devices in the modernising ecosystem. Managing the distribution of devices across networks and the application landscape can be a complicated task. There is a need for a dynamic increase or decrease in capacity, coupled with vertical and horizontal scalability and extendibility of the solutions. Scalability and capacity requirements need to be documented in the non-functional requirements document and matched to the solution building blocks. We need to be mindful that these requirements must be traceable to each modernisation solution building block. A solution building block is the smallest unit of the solution from functionality perspectives.

Modernisation Use Cases

To further improve the requirements, we need to start collecting and analysing solution use cases. As Enterprise Architects, we must help the solution and domain architects to obtain, analyse, understand and validate the modernisation use cases. The validated use cases can be very beneficial for requirement validation and making architectural decisions.

A use case is a specific situation in which a product or service in a solution to be used by the consumers. We develop the use cases from the users' perspective. We need to understand how the consumers are intended to be using a particular component or aspect of the solution. Usually, the functional requirements can help us to formulate the use cases; or, in some circumstances, use cases help formulate the Functional Requirements. This means that the use cases and solution requirements are interrelated. We need to analyse use cases and requirements together; not in isolation.

Some selected users can help us understand the use cases when we interact with them. We need to ask the users questions and obtain their feedback on how they are intended to use a function that is expected to be in the modernisation solution documents.

In general, overall solution use cases need to be defined and elaborated with the input of all stakeholders of the solution, not just end-users. There may be different use cases for different stakeholders.

Use cases can also be determined based on the roles and personas involves in developing a solution. Personas represent fictitious characters, which are based on our knowledge of the users in the solution. Identifying personas and the use of them in our use case development and requirements analysis can be very beneficial. Agile methods have a strong focus on the use of personas.

Once the use cases are understood, precisely documented, and approved by all the relevant stakeholders, the requirements can be more explicit, decisions can be made more effectively, and the solution building blocks can be developed with more confidence.

Trade-offs

Modernisation architectures require making trade-offs to reach optimal solution outcomes. When making trade-offs, we need to consider several crucial factors, such as cost, quality, functionality, usability and many other non-functional items within our scope and roadmap.

We can define a trade-off as creating a balance between two required yet incompatible items. In other words, a trade-off is a compromise between two options. It is possible to make a trade-off between quality and cost for particular items. For example, in a solution, we may need to define the interfaces of an application, such as one way or bi-directional, and make required trade-offs for each option to reach the desired goal. To enhance usability, we may consider pre-built widgets for the dashboards as a trade-off for cost.

We must make architectural trade-offs for dealing with uncertainties. For these types of trade-offs, techniques such as comparing, and contrasting can be beneficial. Our trade-offs must be crystal clear to the sponsoring executives explicitly highlighting financial and commercial implications.

Reference Architectures

A reference architecture is a re-usable solution or a design in a template format. The use of a reference architecture for modernisation solutions can save us a considerable amount of time. Reference architectures are developed by experienced solution architects based on successful outcomes obtained from delivered solutions.

This means that we can trust the reference architectures as they were once successfully delivered. Following the same path as our customised specifications, these re-usable templates can save us a considerable amount of time and can improve the quality of our solutions.

As reference architectures are developed by experienced architects, they can also guide us in dealing with the unknown aspects of the solutions. Reference architectures can be used for various domains, can be combined to extend functionality and can be integrated for the final architecture solutions.

Reference architectures are developed based on the collaborative spirit in many organisations. Some architects share their experiences internally or externally for various reasons. For example, some architects share them for charitable give-back purposes or networking, or to boost their reputation and recognition in their industry. Whatever the reasons they share them, the reference architectures are invaluable resources for our planned solution architectures.

Open-source organisations produce many reference architectures in their domains. There are two primary sources for these reference architectures: either their members develop them as part of an open-source team, or some commercial companies donate their re-usable assets to the open-source organisations as reference architectures. The Open Group (TOG) is a typical example of this kind of open-source organisation.

Reference Architectures can be at a high-level or other detailed levels. A typical IoT reference Architecture at a high level can include essential points, such as Portal, Dashboard, API Management, Analytics, Services, Communications, Devices, Device Management, Security Management, Infrastructure and so on. Reference Architectures are usually represented in diagrams with minimal text to explain the representations in the diagrams. Clarity is the main factor for a reference architecture. Reference Architectures usually are easy to understand and use.

As Enterprise Architects, we need to encourage our domain and solution architects to leverage available references architectures related to enterprise modernisation and transformation initiatives. We also need to encourage them to create their reference architectures and share with other domain architects in the enterprise. From my experience, smart reuse can help reduce enterprise cost substantially.

High-Level Designs and Models

Enterprise modernisations initiatives require the development of multiple high-level designs and models. Use of several architectural models can be instrumental.

Some of the vital Architectural models which we can apply to the potential modernisation solutions are Component

Model, Operational Model, Performance Model, Security Model, Availability Model, Services Model and Cost Model. These models need to be precisely documented, reviewed by the domain architects and governed by the Architecture Board or a Design Authority in the organisation.

Documentation of the architectural models can include both textual explanations and practical diagrams. For example, for a Component Model, all components and their relationships can be clearly illustrated in a diagram. The components and their functions can also be explained in detail. The diagrams can be useful communication tools for the models because the governance process for handling the solution architecture models requires presenting them to the Architecture Board or a Design Authority. With effective communication, obtaining technical assurance approvals can be faster and easier.

Approval for some of these models may also need to be obtained from the financial, commercial and other business stakeholders. For example, the Cost Model, Services Model and Availability Model can have content that requires financial approval. Let's remember that we not only deal with the architectural and technical aspect of the modernisation solution but also the financial and commercial aspects.

As Enterprise Architects, we usually don't create models or high-level designs, but we know their importance and guide the other architects using the best architectural practices. We ensure that the high-level designs are produced using our strategy and roadmap and fully aligned for reaching optimal solutions goals.

Detailed Designs and Specifications

Like any other enterprise IT system, modernisation and transformation solutions are expected to deliver all their specifications correctly. Comprehensive configuration management for solutions can be effective and useful when dealing with specifications.

In modernisation solutions, a specification can be defined as the act of precisely identifying the enterprise ecosystem items. Since specifications require precision, delivering the right specification is an essential requirement for enterprise applications and their associated critical business and emergency responses.

In modernisation solutions, system specifications need to be accurate, reliable and fast when collecting data, communicating information, sharing data and making accurate decisions. Unreliable communication of the specifications by various silos, inaccurate decisions made by those specifications, their cumbersome layout can lead to disastrous results when attempting to detail the modernisation solutions.

Finding the wrong specifications during the implementation and production support phase can be very cost-prohibitive due to massive re-work requirements. In addition to rework, the implications for SLAs can also cause a considerable amount of financial loss to the organisation.

As Enterprise Architects, we set and chair the design authority for the modernisation and transformation programs within our responsibility area. We must closely work with the solution architects and the solution designers. We cannot afford any silos in high level and detail design phase. It must be a fully integrated and collaborative team under our technical and architectural leadership. This is a critical success factor for enterprise modernisation and transformation solutions.

Chapter Summary and Key Points

Enterprise modernisation is a long journey moving the

enterprise from chaos to coherence.

Both a top-down and bottom-up approach can be applied. At the top tier business, IT processes and at the bottom tier IT infrastructure.

We need to manage scope efficiently and reflect the reality using some estimates for resourcing and timelines leveraging the skills of project, program and financial managers.

The solution strategy process provides an objective assessment of the current situation. It aligns the program goals with the organisational goals at the enterprise level and ensures that all gaps are covered.

By using the strategy and considering the dependencies Enterprise Architects develop a high-level roadmap to inform the sponsoring executives.

Modernisation roadmap can include the current state at a high level, the future state, major transformational goals, and indicate the key outcomes, timelines and a ballpark cost for the overall modernisation.

Enterprise modernisation viability assessment must include key risks, constraints, and dependencies at the enterprise level. These items need to be organised adequately to make sense for the executive stakeholders.

After requirements are collected and analysed at a reasonable amount, the next important activity is to prioritise the requirements based on business impact.

Enterprise Architects need to develop criteria to prioritise the requirements based on factors depicted in the strategy and roadmap documents, as well as the financial and business priorities set by the sponsoring executives.

A use case is a specific situation in which a product or service in a solution to be used by the consumers. We develop the use cases from the users' perspective.

We can define a trade-off as creating a balance between two required yet incompatible items. In other words, a trade-off is a compromise between two options.

A reference architecture is a re-usable solution or a design in a template format. The use of a reference architecture for modernisation solutions can save us a considerable amount of time.

Enterprise modernisations initiatives require the development of multiple high-level designs and models. Use of several architectural models can be instrumental.

Finding the wrong specifications during the implementation and production support phase can be very cost-prohibitive due to massive re-work requirements. In addition to rework, the implications of SLAs can also cause a considerable amount of financial loss to the organisation.

We must closely work with the solution architects and the solution designers. We cannot afford any silos in high level and detail design phase. It must be a fully integrated and collaborative team under our technical and architectural leadership.

Chapter 4: Redefining Roles & Responsibilities of Enterprise Architect for Modern World

Purpose

In this section, we explore and redefine the vital roles, responsibilities, and accountabilities of Enterprise Architects within modernisation and transformation contexts. The points provided in the subsequent sections are not job roles, position titles or general duties. These points help us recognise the critical role of Enterprise Architects, specifically for modernising the enterprise.

Let me highlight that we are not focussing on creating a brand-new enterprise architecture. We are trying to modernise an established enterprise architecture to meet growing consumer demands, create new business insights, generate new business opportunities, and potential revenue streams.

In the following sections, we also touch on the day to day activities and interactions of Enterprise Architects to empower the modernisation programs and associated solution goals for planned strategic success.

Architecture and Design Responsibilities for Modernisation Lifecycle

Applying a rigorous enterprise architecture approach is a critical aspect of modernisation initiatives. Let's beware that if the enterprise architecture process goes wrong in a modernisation initiative, everything else goes wrong. All other architecture types, such as solution architecture, system architecture, integration architecture, and other architecture domains, are all dependent on the quality of enterprise architecture. Apart from architecture, the subsequent activities in the modernisation life cycle are also adversely affected.

After a validated, business-focused, and pragmatic architecture supporting the modernisation strategy, the design (both high level and detailed level) is the next vital aspect to be considered in the modernisation lifecycle. Therefore, Enterprise Architects also perform the role of a Design Authority at the enterprise level. However, this does not mean that Enterprise Architects perform design activities. Far from it! They cannot cope with a myriad of design activities. There may be multiple architects and solution designs for various components. The role of Enterprise Architects is to supervise the design using a Design Authority structure.

A Design Authority consists of multiple architects with diverse expertise in different domains. Enterprise Architects are like a symphony orchestra leader. Similarly, Enterprise Architects orchestrate the activities with their broad knowledge and understanding of the strategy, architecture, technical matters, and business. They govern the Design Authority by using their organisational skills coupled with other architectural skills and business understanding.

Enterprise Architects must have strategic, architectural thinking, and design thinking skills. These esteemed architects need to articulate the current enterprise environment to the sponsoring senior executives, set future enterprise environment goals, and show how to bridge the gap for modernisation goals between these two environments.

At a high level, Enterprise Architects must understand the overall modernisation scope for enterprise, modernisation requirements, and use cases of the modernisation solutions. Besides, Enterprise Architects need to perform Viability Assessments which are critical to enterprise modernisation programs. These architects must regularly assess risks, issues, dependencies and constraints considering strengths, weaknesses, opportunities and threats in their day to day tasks.

Dynamic and Flexible Governance

Enterprise Architects are responsible and accountable for architectural and technical governance. Technical governance is an essential aspect of modernisation initiatives. The modernisation programs require particular governance model due to their nature. A dynamic and flexible governance model is essential for modernisation initiatives. The traditional stringent and extreme rule-based oppressive governance models can be roadblocks to the progress. Agility principles best suit to the dynamic governance models.

Enterprise Architects usually perform the role of technical governance head in sizeable modernisation programs. They can have formal governance roles. For example, these architects can run the architecture review boards or design authority forums established for complex modernisation programs.

One of the common frameworks for technical governance in the industry is COBIT (Control Objectives for Information and related Technology). Use of frameworks like COBIT can help organisations gain optimal value from their IT investments by maintaining a balance between gaining benefits and optimising risk levels and resource use. There can be other governance model based on the industry which enterprise belongs and adheres.

Technical Distinction

Enterprise Architects performing modernisation programs must have distinct technology expertise covering a broad spectrum of technologies in all IT domains. They must be technically eminent professionals. Technical eminence refs to outstanding technical expertise recognised internally and externally to the organisation of a technical leader who is influential and high impact to both technical and business communities.

Professional and technical eminence for Enterprise Architects requires not only expertise in technical and architectural areas but also all associated and related domains in a broader scope. Enterprise Architects must have strong industry skills, demonstrate thought leadership, and possess multiple domain expertise. These architects are highly regarded and sought after for their views and contributions to modernisation initiatives.

Leading the enterprise for modernisation requires distinguishing factors in multiple technology domains with broad and deep understanding to some extent. Technical eminence and professional distinction are prerequisites for Enterprise Architects.

Business and Technical Communication

Enterprise Architects need to speak both business and technical language in modernisation engagements. They need to communicate the business vision, strategy, plans, goals, and benefits of enterprise architecture efforts across all IT organisations and lines of business. They also communicate architecture strategy, goals, and objectives to increase awareness throughout the enterprise on an ongoing basis.

Exceptional communication skills are essential for Enterprise Architects dealing with modernisation initiatives. Their communication skills are well respected and sought after by their peers, managers, and customers. They are expected to communicate at all levels with confidence and ease. They must articulate the most complex situations and technical matters to all stakeholders in a language that those people can understand. Enterprise Architect must customise their messages based on audience profile.

Enterprise Architects also need to encourage their team members to communicate clearly and effectively to share their knowledge in the architecture team or outside of the immediate teams. Enterprise Architects are expected to be communication mentors and coaches. They need to observe their team members and provide constructive feedback for their communication capabilities.

Enterprise Architects must particularly articulate sophisticated technology matters and tools to both technical people in necessary details and succinctly to the business stakeholders using the right terms and references with clarity.

Innovation Catalyst

Enterprise Architects must be innovators and innovation catalysts. They need to be creative and original thinkers. These architects continuously need to combine, compare and contrast things to create new meanings, new understandings, new use cases, and new value propositions.

To some extent, in modernisation agendas, these architects also need to be inventive and preferably become inventors. They need to look at the things from a novelty perspective. These architects must create new values for old concepts, terms or ideas. They must look at things from different angles. This inventive thinking is an essential requirement of achieving modernisation goals in enterprises.

Enterprise Architects must understand the value of innovation. They need to become a catalyst for innovation and keep innovating relentlessly. These architects must create an innovation culture in the enterprise and embed it to the organisations' ecosystem.

Mentoring and Coaching

Mentoring and coaching is a cultural shift and the essential requirement of modernising environments. There must be a constant nurturing and knowledge transfer from top to bottom. To this end, Enterprise Architects must be mentors for their team members, other team members, people from partnering organisations, students from universities, and even external people in other organisations. They need to generously share their knowledge and transfer them to anyone who needs such knowledge to utilise in modernisations engagements.

These architects also need to be good at coaching their peers, subordinates, and cross-team members by being a soundboard to them. Junior team members can be easily overwhelmed by the rapid pace and changes of modernisation programs. I observed that some distinguished Enterprise Architects are excellent listeners and even contribute to wellbeing of their team members providing coaching sessions for stressful colleagues resulting in therapeutic outcomes. These are well respected and sought-after leaders who make real cultural shifts for meeting the demands of modernisation goals in large organisations.

Enterprise Architects need to provide technical mentorship to other managers and executives who are not as technologically savvy struggling with complex demands of modernisation initiatives. Their mentoring and coaching capabilities can help non-technical team members to stretch themselves to bigger and better roles in the enterprise. They can coach these non-technical team members as one on one basis or in groups. Mentoring and coaching must be a continuous activity in enterprise modernisation programs.

Change Catalyst

Change is critical for enterprise modernisation. Everything changes continuously and rapidly. Change leadership is a vital function for modernisation. Dealing with rapid change is non-trivial, and indeed require delicate skills, experience, and insights.

Enterprise Architects must be catalysts for ongoing change. With their catalytical contributions, they need to refresh the culture to more agile, collaborative, inventive, and innovative landscapes in the enterprise.

These architects must create innovative sets of practices in the ecosystem. Their attributes, such as being responsive, sharing and learning mutually, and having fun with joy in a pleasant team environment, can have a tremendous impact on improving the culture for positive change.

New Way of Learning

Learning is a never-ending process in transformational environments leading towards modernisation of legacy enterprise. Due to changing technologies, process and tools, Enterprise Architects and their colleagues responsible from other architectural aspects need to learn rapidly and efficiently. Enterprise Architects can have a wide variety of learning styles. Based on situations and conditions, they need to learn formally and informally based on circumstances. They must turn every possible interaction to a potential learning opportunity.

Enterprise Architects must create learning opportunities for themselves and their team members. They also need to teach other people actively and on-demand. By teaching their team members, they even learn more and better. This new way of learning is critical to meet the demands of enterprise modernisation goals.

Talent Support

Talent is essential in enterprise modernisation solutions. Therefore, Enterprise Architects need to understand the value and importance of talent for modernisation programs. Without calibre talent, enterprise modernisation programs cannot progress productively.

To this end, Enterprise Architects need to be very cautious to nurture and keep talent in their teams. They need to make every effort to retain valuable talent in their teams. We cannot emphasise enough that talent is a crucial enabler of core products and services of modernising enterprises. Without talent, an organisation cannot be competitive in its modernisation goals. There is a constant talent hunting in the industry to secure these scarce resources.

To conclude, Enterprise Architects need to perform talent management and facilitation roles. They must encourage the less junior team members to perform better and turn them into talented team players. These architects also need to pick up poor performance in the team and help remove poorly performing employees and replace them with talented team members who can genuinely contribute to the modernisation vision.

High-Performance Teams

Enterprise Modernisation requires team members who can perform and produce at the highest possible level. These team members must perform optimally at all times to meet the challenges of modernisation programs. Their skills and capabilities must be tested and validated to suit the type of work they are performing.

Building high-performance teams are critical for the success of enterprise modernisation. Enterprise Architects must create collaborative, well-functioning, and high performing teams to run successful digital transformation initiatives.

These experienced architects need to create proactive and engaged local technical teams and community of practices as give back activities. These high-quality teams and collaborative community of practices can generate innovative, high-quality solutions in agility. They are ideal contributors to modernisation, digital transformation, and fusion goals.

Blind Spots Detectors

People have blind spots all the time. It is a natural and inevitable situation. Blind spots can be hazardous in many circumstances, especially in modernisation initiatives. The owner of the blind spot cannot see his or her blind spot unless using specific tools or assistance from someone else who is more experienced.

Habits and habitual thinking patterns are common causes of blind spots. Focusing on details without seeing the big picture can also cause cloudy thinking and ultimately dangerous blind spots. However, Enterprise Architects are astute and professional observers. They need to look for big pictures from multiple angles and deep dive when needed hence can quickly identify blind spots and weaknesses experienced by their team members.

Enterprise Architects need to articulate situations with constructive feedback, lots of clarifying examples, metaphors, and similes. This influential articulation focus can help people to see their blind spots, understand their weaknesses, and turn them into strengths. Related to blind spots, identifying hidden agendas and hidden costs are critical for enterprise modernisation initiatives.

Taking Measures

Taking necessary measures are essential for enterprise modernisation. Enterprise Architects need to focus on both qualitative and quantitative measures for team success. These architects can manage across complex matrix structures in their organisations. As metric oriented professionals, Enterprise Architects need to use KPIs (Key Performance Indicators). They must use a team dashboard to see the trends and qualify and quantify progress in visual formats for the team members and the business stakeholders.

Enterprise Architects also need to encourage other team members to create their dashboard and shared dashboard for the team. They must turn the enterprise to a data-driven organisation to measure the progress of modernisation goals structurally and methodically.

One of the key measures is customer orientation and support mechanisms. These architects ensure a customer-centric outlook is provided, focusing on continually improving client experience with measurable results.

Thought Leadership

Enterprise Architects must be the 'thought leaders'. Thought leadership is a critical need and demand in modernisation environments, for changing cultures, and transforming ecosystems. Enterprise Architects, as thought leaders, are excellent technical leaders in modernising enterprises.

These architects need to think digitally. In other words, they need to be digital thought leaders to achieve modernisation goals. In the past, we used to call them technology-minded leaders. We now use the term of digital thinkers or digital thought leaders. Some also call them digital opinion leaders. The vital point in this context is to be a role model by practising digital trends.

Enterprise Architects need to be drivers of ubiquitous digital transformations at a personal and organisational level. As almost every organisation nowadays have some modernisation program to some extent, Enterprise Architects leading these businesses must think digitally. They must be thought leaders and at the forefront of digital modernisation initiatives.

Outcome Creator

Tangible outcomes are essential for the success of enterprise modernisation. Modernisation programs require tangible outcomes iteratively rather than monolithic. For example, some tangible outcomes can be a virtualisation of platforms, creating containers, creating reusable shared resources, reviewed products, and agreed services.

Enterprise Architects need to pay special attention to providing tangible outcomes with the support of their team members. The modernising environment presents a constant and rapid change and any change matters in the transforming ecosystem.

These small and rapid changes lead to more significant tangible outcomes at later stages of the modernisation; for example, the systems may need to be fully automated, loosely coupled, service-oriented, software-defined, self-learning, self-managing, and self-healing are a few to mention in this context.

Professional Background

As of last but not least, Enterprise Architects need to come from deep technical backgrounds and specialist level experience starting as a technical junior. Enterprise Architects coming from a technical background can be much different from other architects coming from a management background with limited technical knowledge, skills and experience. While both types of architects have value for the business, the dynamics can be very different from innovation, agility, collaboration, and technical excellence perspectives.

My observations reveal that selected Enterprise Architects from extensive technical background coupled with excellent business and people skills can be more productive and effective in complex modernisation environments. Those architects coming from strong technical backgrounds can be exceptional hands-on architects.

Ironically, not every technical person can be a competent Enterprise Architect. Therefore, we need to explore the attributes that make a technical person an excellent Enterprise Architect. With all due respect to the architects coming from the advanced management and leadership schools or other academic environments with years of experience, my observations revealed that most of these skilful people are true leaders, however, in general, they are not necessarily ideal candidates to be Enterprise Architects to make a real difference for substantial modernisation initiatives in the enterprise. Of course, there are self-taught management professionals with remarkable passion in technology who constitute the exceptions in some cases for leading complex modernisation initiatives in large enterprises.

Chapter Summary and Key Points

Applying a rigorous enterprise architecture approach is a critical aspect of modernisation initiatives.

In addition to chairing Architecture Review Board, Enterprise Architects also perform the role of a Design Authority at the enterprise level.

Enterprise Architects must have strategic, architectural thinking, and design thinking skills.

Enterprise Architects must understand the overall modernisation scope for enterprise, modernisation requirements, and use cases of the modernisation solutions.

Enterprise Architects must regularly assess risks, issues, dependencies and constraints considering strengths, weaknesses, opportunities and threats to support enterprise modernisation initiatives.

A dynamic and flexible governance model is essential for modernisation initiatives. The traditional stringent and extreme rule-based oppressive governance models can be roadblocks to the progress.

Enterprise Architects performing modernisation programs must have technical eminence and distinct technology expertise covering a broad spectrum of technologies in all IT domains.

Enterprise Architects need to communicate the business vision, strategy, plans, goals, and benefits of enterprise architecture efforts across all IT organisations and lines of business.

Enterprise Architects must articulate the most complex situations and technical matters to all stakeholders in a language that those people can understand by customising messages based on audience profile.

Enterprise Architects must be innovators and innovation catalysts. They need to be creative and original thinkers.

Enterprise Architects need to provide architectural and technical mentorship to all stakeholders in the enterprise.

Enterprise Architects must be catalysts for ongoing change. With their catalytical contributions, they need to refresh the culture to more agile, collaborative, inventive, and innovative landscapes in the enterprise.

As active leaders and teachers, Enterprise Architects must create innovative learning opportunities for themselves and their team members.

Enterprise Architects need to perform talent management and facilitation roles. They need to be very cautious to nurture and retain valuable talent in their teams.

Building high-performance teams are critical for the success of enterprise modernisation. Enterprise Architects must create collaborative, well-functioning, and high performing teams to run successful digital transformation initiatives.

Enterprise Architects need to articulate situations with constructive feedback, lots of clarifying examples, metaphors, and similes. This influential articulation focus can help people to see their blind spots, understand their weaknesses, and turn them into strengths.

In modernisation programs, Enterprise Architects need to use Key Performance Indicators. They must use team dashboards to see the trends and qualify and quantify progress in visual formats for the team members and the business stakeholders.

Thought leadership is a critical need and demand in modernisation environments, for changing cultures, and transforming ecosystems.

Enterprise Architects need to pay special attention to providing tangible outcomes with the support of their team members. The modernising environment presents a constant and rapid change and any change matters in the transforming ecosystem.

Chapter 5: Innovative Agility & Fusion for Modern Enterprise

Purpose

In this section, we aim to understand the importance of innovation as an empowering factor for enterprise modernisation. I attempt to provide my observations and thoughts on how Enterprise Architects can use innovation coupled with collaboration and principles of fusion-focused approach to initiate, empower, and deliver enterprise modernisation goals. Let's start by defining innovation in this context.

Definition of Innovation

We can define innovation in different terms based on the type of work, professions, industry, and other backgrounds. In this book, my definition of innovation is the use of creativity for generating new ideas, new methods, new approaches, new techniques, new processes, and new tools or improve the current environment to gain insights, add business value, reduce costs, and increase revenue.

Innovation relates to novelty, improvement, iterations, and ongoing steady progress. Innovative thinking generates novel ideas, focuses on improving ideas, and strives for making iterative progress. To this end, innovation is closely related to Agile delivery principles.

Innovation and technical excellence are tightly coupled and interrelated. Innovation ignites technical excellence, and technical excellence enables innovation. Therefore, Enterprise Architects must be natural innovators. They need to practice innovation in their daily life and motivate people around them to innovate constantly.

Innovation feeds the culture and is a critical aspect of a modernising ecosystem in organisations. Enterprise cultures embracing innovation can naturally renew themselves for surviving and thriving in fluctuating conditions which are typical in modernising enterprise. These enterprises extend to the next generations with constant progress, renewed image, improved services, and stronger capabilities.

Innovative Thinking

Innovation starts with thinking differently. Innovative thinking requires multiple modes of thinking. Traditionally, most of us think vertically, linearly or in binary. We usually use vertical and linear types of thinking for problem-solving. Applying logic and streamlining thoughts are some techniques in this type of thinking mode. Linear thinking goes deep down, layer by layer, and in a logical manner. Binary thinking consists of simple terms such as yes or no, black and white, good or bad.

As opposed to vertical thinking, horizontal thinking covering more breadth rather than depth which was also coined as 'lateral thinking' by Edward de Bono is a type of thinking aiming to generate unpredictable ideas by breaking out the rigid thought patterns. Lateral thinking challenges the assumptions. It looks for alternatives and goes beyond the ordinary, creating radical solutions.

The horizontal type of thinking is beneficial for creating innovations. There are different techniques that we can use for horizontal thinking. Some commonly used techniques for horizontal thinking are randomisations, distortions, reversals, exaggerations, metaphors, analogies, dreaming, theme mining, questioning the norms, and creating contradictions.

One of the practical techniques that Enterprise Architects need to use is mind mapping. They must articulate their thoughts using representative maps on paper or a whiteboard. They also need to use other visual representations, such as drawing pictures on a whiteboard while explaining abstract ideas. People can visualise abstract ideas better by looking at the drawings. I know that many Enterprise Architects in my teams have excellent drawing skills. They prove that the proverbial one picture tells a thousand words.

Innovation Culture and Ecosystem

Many enterprises create an innovation culture embedded in their modernising ecosystem. Enterprise Architects are the catalyst for the formation and maintenance of the innovation culture. With the support of their technical leaders, team members of these cultures continually challenge the status quo. People embrace changes and challenges in innovative cultures.

In these modernising organisations, innovation becomes habitual. Team members strive for excellence by creating innovations in their day to day tasks. No one is called weird names or other judgemental adjectives. Instead, innovation is welcomed, praised, and even awarded in different ways. People embrace constant change, even if it is painful at times. They learn how to turn the pain to pleasure with the rewarding results of evident transformations.

People collaborate better in innovative cultures. They see themselves with the changing conditions in new positions. They do not resist as they know that change can be useful for them. In these innovative cultures, they have excellence centres or ideation labs. They perform ongoing trials and errors to create and test new ideas. They may fail at times, but they fail quickly and come back to reality with improved knowledge. They see the failing tests as new definitions.

Enterprise Architects must be catalysts for innovations.

They need to support the innovative culture and water the innovation garden regularly to survive and thrive. They not only must innovate but also enable others to innovate.

How to Ignite Innovation in Modernising Enterprise

Harnessing and driving creative thinking result in innovation. For Enterprise Architects, innovation must turn to habit or more accurately a lifestyle. These leaders need to understand the importance of innovation for digital transformation and modernisation goals and inspire their followers to be innovative as well. The best way for Enterprise Architects to ignite innovation is to be a role model for their followers. They need to encourage the team members to innovate, and they reward them for their innovative achievements.

To ignite innovation, Enterprise Architects must consider market conditions, client needs, and map them organisation's capabilities then define the focus areas for innovation agenda to enable digital transformation.

One of the methods Enterprise Architects need to use is the design thinking activities which take place daily in the team interactions. Design thinking allows the team to be intuitive and logical at the same time. Design thinking enables team members to be more creative to recognise new patterns. As design thinking is closely associated with the Agile methods, the design thinking professionals progress their ideas iteratively. Enterprise modernisation initiatives require the adoption of design thinking to its core culture.

Innovation as a Mindset

Enterprise Architects need to have a growth mindset to ignite innovation. They must help their team members with a fixed mindset to convert to a growth mindset as it is an essential factor to survive and thrive in modernising enterprise. Growth mindset leading towards innovation must be a build-in characteristic in the personalities of Enterprise Architects.

Metaphorically, it is like air and water for their survival. In addition to survival, these architects also need to use innovation for thriving. Enterprise Architects not only need to create innovation at a personal level but also through collaboration with the immediate teams and extended teams. They must keep asking how to deliver innovative experiences moment by moment continuously.

Enterprise Architects must lead to a mindset shift in small and large teams. They must hold a positive 'can do' attitude for any challenges they have. They must be customer-centric and put themselves in customers' shoes with strong empathy. Using design thinking techniques, they can develop empathy maps. Enterprise Architects and their team members must analyse the personas using empathy maps. This mindset is part of the design thinking practice mentioned in previous sections.

Recognising Hurdles for Innovation

It is critical to recognise innovation blockers and show stoppers. The roadblocks to innovation can be in various forms and from various angles. One of the main showstoppers is keeping the status quo. Traditional enterprises and business processes maintain the status quo. There is a strong resistance to change in these cultures.

Many organisations nowadays recognise the importance of innovation. However, there is always a hidden fear and resistance towards innovation by some people who may have hidden agendas. Enterprise Architects must recognise those people who try to sabotage innovation in the modernisation programs. Even though these people with a negative mindset may be in the minority, they still can have a tremendous adverse impact on innovation in organisations.

One way of dealing with these innovation stoppers are to be transparent to them and have a close face to face conversations. Enterprise Architects find ways to engage those types of people and show the value and benefit of innovation to these types of people. If those people can see the value for themselves, then they can be converted to innovation supporters. The critical point is asking them and making them think positively.

The business as usual mentality can be a roadblock for innovation. Cumbersome business processes and tired employees can hardly have any interest in innovation as they cannot see the immediate need. The best way is to separate innovation and business as usual as two different departments. Of course, business, as usual, is essential for the organisation to continue its current function but these organisations also need innovation for transforming to the digital world for new insights, market competitiveness, and revenue generation. Modernisation programs must be kept separate from the business as usual practices.

Chapter Summary and Key Points

Innovation starts with thinking differently. Innovative thinking requires multiple modes of thinking.

Some commonly used techniques for horizontal thinking are randomisations, distortions, reversals, exaggerations, metaphors, analogies, dreaming, theme mining, questioning the norms, and creating contradictions.

As innovation catalysts for modernisation, Enterprise Architect need to support the innovative culture and water the innovation garden regularly to survive and thrive.

To ignite innovation, Enterprise Architects must consider market conditions, client needs, and map them organisation's capabilities then define the focus areas for innovation agenda to enable digital transformation.

As customer-centric professionals, Enterprise Architects must lead to a mindset shift in small and large teams. They must hold a positive 'can do' attitude for any challenges they have.

Enterprise Architects must recognise those people who try to sabotage innovation in the modernisation programs. Even though these people with a negative mindset may be in the minority, they still can have a tremendous adverse impact on innovation in organisations.

Chapter 6: Simplifying Architecture for Modern Enterprise

Purpose

Simplicity is a crucial pillar in our framework. Simplicity can empower enterprise modernisation. Simplicity is a substantial factor affecting digital transformations and modernisation programs. Simplicity is also one of the critical attributes of Enterprise Architects. These architects strive for simplicity. They must be capable of turning complexity to simplicity. Managing complexity is an essential skill that Enterprise Architects must possess.

Simplicity touches almost every angle of modernisation solution as they are incredibly involved with complexity. Therefore, I dedicated a chapter to highlight the importance and necessity of the simplicity pillar. Let's start exploring simplicity by defining it to reach a common understanding.

Meaning of Simplicity

Simplicity, in sophisticated enterprises, is a paradoxical topic. One may ask how to expect complicated modernisations to be provided with simplicity as this type of activity refers to complexity. Yes, modernisation is a complex topic and requires sophisticated attributes such as in-depth knowledge, varied skills, and extensive experience. The point is using these sophisticated attributes we must simplify the complicated processes, systems, tools and technologies.

Ironically, to create simplicity, one needs to deal with a lot of complexity, complications and sophisticated matters. Obtaining the required knowledge, acquiring advanced skills, and gaining substantial experience are not easy and not indeed simple activities. Paradoxically, we need to deal with complexity to create simplicity.

However, one who deals with complexity and sophisticated matters can also have extraordinary attributes to simplify things for other people. Creating simplicity to communicate effectively with others is an essential leadership attribute for Enterprise Architects.

Simplicity is a well sought-after characteristic in IT services and products. The modern digital world is formed for simplicity for consumers. As opposed to complexity, simplicity is favourable by consumers. Therefore, technical leaders are expected to simplify complex situations and complicated problems and offer simple solutions.

Enterprise Architects can articulate the most complicated and complex matters in a simple format that is understandable by others. However, simplicity requires in-depth knowledge and flexible thinking. Simplicity also refers to clear communication. One way of clear communication is to customise our message to people's level and the right context we communicate.

Simplicity is a desired attribute not only for communication but also for dealing with technical matters and building relationships. Enterprise Architects must communicate in simple terms. They need to simplify technical matters when dealing with technical issues. They must establish relationships that depict simplicity and efficiency.

Enterprise Architects must be consumer-centric and ask the question of how we can create products and services simple, intuitive, and human-centric. The consumer-oriented simplicity is a requirement for leading innovative teams in the modernisation initiatives. Enterprise Architects, with this capability, need to motivate their teams to think in simple terms when conveying their messages for complicated technical processes.

The path to enterprise modernisation begins with simplifying the systems, tools, technology, and process components at all levels and layers. One of the effective ways to this simplification is automating routine tasks and repetitive technology stacks. Automation can help to simplify. Enterprise Architects, while delving into details in technology, they also need to focus on emerging needs by simplifying them in consumer terms.

Process Simplicity

Consumers keep complaining that technology creates complexity and make it difficult to understand concepts and objects in natural human language. For example, many consumers complain about the cumbersome documentation written in a convoluted language. They also show their disapproval for voluminous of documents for the use of a small technology device. They call it a waste.

There is a generational disconnect in dealing with process simplicity. The old generation used to read manuals to solve their computer problems. Software stacks used to come with large read-me files. However, the new generation works with technology intuitively. They hardly look at product manuals. If they are stuck, they would usually watch a YouTube video on how to do something or how to troubleshoot something. Instead of reading, they prefer watching a video. This is a dramatic cultural shift in consumer technologies.

Enterprise Architect leading modernisation programs need to have a mission to simplify the business and technology processes and make them user-centric. This effort aims at efficiency and effectiveness of technology product and services leading to modernisation and digital transformations.

Service Simplicity

Technology is rapidly transforming towards service orientation. Most of the technology domains are provided based on services models. The most common technology trend is the Cloud services model. In the Cloud services model, everything is provided as services. For example, cloud service models can be infrastructure, platform, and software as a service. Indeed, many other technology stacks such as Business Processes and Big Data can be offered as a service.

The services model requires substantial amounts of simplification for users to take benefits of using technologies. Enterprise Architects using their skills to simplify services, can add value to the business. They inspire their team members to simplify everything by empathising with consumers. Simplification is an innovative process that Enterprise Architects must lead as role models.

Simplicity and clarity are closely related. Especially in the technical services industry, providing a transparent experience to the technical team members can be very beneficial. Besides, making this transparent experience available to the end-user even more simplified and more explicit formats for the usage patterns can add additional value to the service provision goals.

The best way of providing simplicity to the consumer is to think like the consumers. Enterprise Architects must keep focusing on the core tenets of simplifying products and services for the best possible user experience and satisfactory consumption merits.

Design Simplicity for Modernisation

Design simplicity is an essential factor to consider in enterprise modernisation goals. Design simplicity has a tremendous impact on the subsequent phases of the modernisation lifecycle, such as service delivery and support. The simpler the design, the more effective the delivery and better service support.

Applying design thinking, combined with adopting agile methods for design, is one of the simplification approaches. Simplification is an enabler for agile service delivery. Agile methods strive for simplifications using an iterative approach. Iterations are simpler than whole chunks.

By applying agile methods to the design phase, complicated requirements are simplified using simple use cases based on personas. Complex systems are deconstructed to smaller parts and dealt with simpler chunks. System relationships are simplified with iterative flows. The simplifying focus is on smaller building blocks.

Most of the technology services nowadays are digitally offered using mobile devices such as tablets and smartphones. Mobile designs must focus on simplicity by removing clutter from screens due to the nature of small screen views. These types of designs must focus on only fundamentally essential objects. These activities are fundamental considerations for enterprise modernisation goals.

Designing complex systems also require simplifications through modular and service-oriented designs. Modularity and modular approaches to complex solutions are essential for simplification, modernisation, and digital transformation. One of the approaches for the modernisation goals can be a domain-based walkthrough of simplifying modules of IT infrastructure, applications, architecture, middleware, security, network, and data domains.

To elaborate on design simplification in the technology domain, let's take containers as an example. Containers break down monolithic interdependent architectures into manageable, and independent components. A container, as a loosely coupled system, is an entire runtime environment in a bundle. It includes dependencies, binaries, libraries, and configuration files. These new techniques and approaches help us simplify the design process.

Enterprise Architects must be conscious of simplicity for design. They need to run workshops to convey the message for the intuitive user-centric designs based on simplicity principles.

Simplicity of Specifications

For many years, time and energy spent on the system and user specification of software and hardware products and services were substantial. They cost an enormous amount of funds for the projects developing the specifications with many talented engineers, technical architects and other technical specialists. However, it became evident that the investment made on these specifications yielded in little gain than expected.

The digital trends, mobile culture and agile approaches made substantial changes in addressing the cumbersome specifications, especially concerning the users or consumers. The deep-down technical details for user specifications were found unnecessary. An interesting approach was proposed by Agile methods and gained attention over a decade now. Agile methods proposed simplifications of cumbersome specifications delivering in user stories format.

User stories are simple templates, including the functionalities, capabilities, and specifications from users or consumers point of view. Developing and understanding the user stories consist of a single page can be much more comfortable and more effective than developing or reading hundreds of pages of specifications in traditional methods.

Simplicity in Technical Communication

Effective communication requires simplification. Enterprise Architects are capable of simplifying communication. The simplification process for communication enables to facilitate understanding of issues, risks and dependencies effectively. Simplified communication is a challenging task, but we can apply it to our day-to-day interactions by using specific rules and techniques. Enterprise Architects can translate complex problems into clear messages that can be acted on, execute with simplicity and agility.

Refraining from convoluted phrases and instead, use of precise language and explicit statements are essential factors in simplifying communication. Even though Enterprise Architects may have an extensive vocabulary and broad range of technical terms, particularly in-depth knowledge of technical matters, they need to be able to use simple language to pass their message to non-technical people's level. For example, they can use different terms and references while speaking to a manager, a secretary, an executive, a salesperson, and a technician. They can customise their message as needed.

While Enterprise Architects can use advanced business terms to senior executives to articulate a point, they need to use deep technical terms to talk with engineers or technical specialists. This awareness, customisation, and flexibility in communication is a crucial characteristic of these architects.

The attention span for our generation is relatively low due to many technical disruptions in our lives. To this end, Enterprise Architects must get the point quickly before losing the attention of people. For example, they may use lively words to illustrate a situation rather than using abstract terms.

Simplicity in written communication is essential too.

People don't have much time and brainpower to understand intricate details in a technical document. The authors in enterprise modernisation initiatives must be sharp and to the point with clear statements. Short sentences are always preferable to improve readability.

The main benefit of simplification for oral and written communication is to pass the desired message effectively in the shortest possible time. It is beneficial to refrain from jargons, big words and complex sentence structures in oral and written communication.

Being able to articulate a situation in the simplest possible terms also can increase the confidence of the target person when dealing with Enterprise Architects. This capability is essential for enterprise modernisation activities.

The right context in simplifying the language is also required. It is essential to balance qualitative and quantitative aspects while conveying a message to the audience. Enterprise Architects are context-aware, and they deliver their message in the right context.

Enterprise Architects need to strive to articulate the business value proposition to the business stakeholders rather than showing off their technical eminence detailing convoluted details.

Governance Simplicity for Modernisation

Complex and complicated governance processes and procedures can be a hurdle for enterprise modernisation initiatives. They can cause delays, confusions, rework and low performance for the modernisation goals. Therefore, it is critical to simplify governance framework, process and procedures for these initiatives.

Enterprise Architects must be aware of the importance of governance and pay special attention to the required rigour.

They cannot compromise the quality requirements in governing technology solutions. However, while having this rigour, they also need to have a balance for delivering the message in the simplest possible terms and making the processes for governance in the most effective ways.

These architects must stay on top of technology trends and developments to govern them for modernisation. As part of their governance role, they need to ensure all technology practices adhere to regulatory standards in their industries.

More Data for Simplicity

Data simplification is a widely discussed topic in all modernising IT environments. One way of simplifying data is to clean data, remove duplications and errors. Reducing data sources and volumes when needed are also used to simplify data management processes.

However, there is a paradoxical situation to point out for data volumes as far as simplicity is concerned for modernisation. For example, more data is believed to create complexity; however, this is not true. It is just the opposite situation. Since we have more data to feed the systems, the systems can produce better output with rich data.

The simplicity can be achieved through the right data analysis, intelligence, powerful tools, and effective management strategies. In other words, when correctly and purposefully analysed, more data can add better intelligence for modernising the data platforms.

Enterprise Architects need to understand the importance of data for modernising initiatives and use established techniques and evolving methods in data science. They can leverage the industry knowledge and focus on simplifying data collection, process, management, storage and analytics.

In addition, for enterprise modernisation, the traditional data management methods cannot suffice; therefore, they need to consider Big Data management technologies, process and tools for this simplification process.

One of the simplified Big Data trends in massive digital transformation and modernisation initiatives is the use of Cloud services for Big Data solutions. There is even a specific Big Data as a Service model. For more information on this topic, you can check my book Architecting Big Data Solutions Integrated with IoT and Cloud available in digital and paper copies.

Simplified Presentations for Effectiveness

There may be many presentations for enterprise modernisation initiatives. Enterprise Architects presents to multiple groups using PowerPoint and Visio images. These architects need to use these tools very carefully to maintain the focus of the audience and effectively convey their critical messages.

Dead from PowerPoint is a famous statement made in all online forums depicting inefficiencies of presentations using tools like PowerPoint. Being brief and concise in presentations is also an essential simplification method for effective communication. For example, we can simplify team presentations by cutting unnecessary, irrelevant details and using a concise number of slides focusing on necessary points when using a PowerPoint as a tool.

Another crucial consideration is focusing on conveying the intended central message rather than trying to impress the audience with sophisticated communication techniques. Endless discussions may cloud the essential message; therefore, it is critical to control the presentation process and focus sharply on the essential points in our presentations.

Enterprise Architects need to provide simplified, clear

and concise presentations without compromising the quality of content and effectiveness of the message. They also need to encourage the team members to follow simplicity principles in their presentations and provide constant constructive feedback to maintain this simplicity culture.

Chapter Summary and Key Points

Simplicity is a crucial pillar in our framework. Simplicity can empower enterprise modernisation. Simplicity is a substantial factor affecting digital transformations and modernisation programs.

Enterprise Architects need to articulate the most complicated and complex matters in a simple format that is understandable by others. However, simplicity requires in-depth knowledge and flexible thinking.

The best way of providing simplicity to the consumer is to think like the consumers. Enterprise Architects must keep focusing on the core tenets of simplifying products and services for the best possible user experience and satisfactory consumption merits.

Design simplicity has a tremendous impact on the subsequent phases of the modernisation lifecycle, such as service delivery and support. The simpler the design, the more effective the delivery and better service support.

Designing complex systems also require simplifications through modular and service-oriented designs. Modularity and modular approaches to complex solutions are essential for simplification, modernisation, and digital transformation.

User stories are simple templates, including the functionalities, capabilities, and specifications from users or consumers point of view.

Refraining from convoluted phrases and instead, use of

precise language and explicit statements are essential factors in simplifying communication. While Enterprise Architects can use advanced business terms to senior executives to articulate a point, they need to use deep technical terms to talk with engineers or technical specialists.

People don't have much time and brainpower to understand intricate details in a technical document. The authors must be sharp and to the point with clear statements. Short sentences are always preferable to improve readability.

Simplicity in written communication is essential too. People don't have much time and brainpower to understand intricate details in a technical document. The authors in enterprise modernisation initiatives must be sharp and to the point with clear statements. Short sentences are always preferable to improve readability.

Complex and complicated governance processes and procedures can be a hurdle for enterprise modernisation initiatives.

The simplicity can be achieved through the right data analysis, intelligence, powerful tools, and effective management strategies. In other words, when correctly and purposefully analysed, more data can add better intelligence for modernising the data platforms.

Being brief and concise in presentations is also an essential simplification method for effective communication. For example, we can simplify team presentations by cutting unnecessary, irrelevant details and using a concise number of slides focusing on necessary points when using a PowerPoint as a tool.

Chapter 7: Agility for Modern Enterprise

Purpose

Agility is our next pillar in this enterprise modernisation framework. Enterprise Architects, in this era, must be agile. This agility can help them to be influential, competitive, and productive in their modernisation engagements. Enterprise Architects must keep asking how they can make their IT footprint more intuitive, responsive, and agile day today. This approach is a foundational requirement of modernisation initiatives. Whist dealing with legacy IT footprint to understand it in an agile manner, Enterprise Architects also need to have the vision of well-functioning modernisation and put their energies on rapid-paced iterative modernisation initiatives.

It is impossible to undertake successful modernisation initiatives with old methods. As this became a reality, many organisations embraced agility and matured in delivering rapidly. Agility is a particular concern for modernisation and digital transformations as consumer demands are increasing based on fast-paced delivery requirements.

Speed to market is one of the most fundamental requirements of businesses nowadays. Agile became the new norm in modernising enterprises. Products are expected to be released faster than they were in the past. Security updates and bug fixes are required more frequently.

Agility affects all aspects of enterprise modernisation. Besides, Enterprise Architects need to act, behave and approach in agility to every aspect of the modernisation solutions. We cover various aspects of agility in the subsequent sections. Let's start with the communication of agility.

How to Communicate Agility

Selling agile nowadays is reasonably easy due to its nature and compelling reasons. Agile is a particular interest to the new generations as they grow with agility in all walks of life. However, the older generation still has a sentimental attachment to waterfall methods. There appears to be some comfort zone created for using waterfall methods.

There is a common perception that Agile methods cut things short hence reduce the quality; however, this is not true. Some agile projects increase the quality due to iterative approaches and checking quality more frequently in every iterative milestone.

Enterprise Architects must articulate the benefits and compelling reasons to use the Agile approach, especially for modernisations leading to digital transformations. It is not feasible to wait and see the end of a gigantic digital transformation project. There are many unknowns; hence, it is not possible to see the end product without constant trial and error in smaller scales for modernisation.

An agile approach allows the team members to test their ideas iteratively. If they fail, they fail quickly and cheaply without costing lots of funds to the initiatives. This business value needs to be understood well and needs to be embedded in the culture of the organisations striving for modernisation goals. Enterprise Architects must be the catalyst for conveying the message and making the necessary cultural adjustments effectively.

How to Ignite and Maintain Agility

Enterprise Architects must be motivators and ignite

agility in enterprise modernisation initiatives. As they are technically capable and business-focused, they need to show the value and share their knowledge and views with team members and other stakeholders.

Enterprise Architects need to actively participate in Agile scrums and provide ongoing feedback and support to the scrum teams. These leaders can also perform the role of the product owner in Agile scrums. As product owners, they can set the acceptance criteria for the product in the allocated modernisation sprint.

Enterprise Architects must develop mental models on how technology users interact with their solution in each iteration. With their action-oriented approach, they must use the backlogs quickly and in priority orders. Furthermore, these architects need to use rewards and recognise the high achievers' effort and contributions for clearing the backlogs in the most effective and innovative ways.

Pragmatic Architecture

In many organisations, due to valid reasons, I observed that architecture creates fear for organisations. In the simplest terms, architecture involves things that are hard to change later. However, this doesn't mean we cannot apply agile to architecture. There is a massive trend to use Agile methods for developing architectural solutions. To address the fear of architecture, I introduce the term pragmatic architecture in fast-paced modernisations initiatives.

Enterprise Architects must take a pragmatic approach to architecture development when engaged in modernisation programs. We know that predicting the future is very hard; therefore, creating an upfront paragon of architecture is not practical. The notion of perfection equates to failure in fast-paced modernisation programs. We cannot afford the use of monolithic Waterfall methods for developing architectures for many months and even years. Taking this extended time is not feasible in this digital age. Consumers expect product and services much quicker than old times.

An iterative approach to architecture can be the most effective investment in the earlier stages of the digital transformation. We can see the architecture development like product development. The iterative method can speed up the architectural process and improve the quality based on the minimally viable product development approach. One way of the pragmatic approach is to use a single domain and apply the learnings to the next domains. This iterative approach can help us progress with confidence and well-managed risk profile.

Rapid Development

After architecture and design, another big topic and concern in modernisation initiatives is development. By using waterfall methods developing a software product used take months and years in the past. Again, consumers cannot wait this long any more. The solution is applying an Agile approach to development. Fortunately, Agile methods are more suited to the development areas in modernisation initiatives.

There are many evolving Agile methods to support different kinds of development processes. Developers embrace Agile methods. They can see the results much more quickly. Use of evolving methods such as DevOps is also prime considerations for enabling modernisation leading to substantial digital transformations.

Enterprise Architects must focus on rapid development and deployment of flexible solutions using Agile methods. They are mindful that speedy time-to-market for digital products is a competitive differentiator in this day and age.

Importance of Automation

Modernisation goals leading to transforming to digital services and delivering products fast to market requires substantial automation activities. Agile methods have a particular focus on automation. Automation enables simplifying and speeding up processes.

Enterprise Architects need to understand the value of automation. Applying automation to modernisation goals, we can reduce the number of resources required to maintain manual and tedious systems. Automation can address human errors and resolve potential errors quickly. Enterprises embracing agile cultures do not resist against automation, in fact, they leverage the capabilities for modernisation goals.

Enterprise Architects must focus on automation and encourage other architects and specialists in their teams to participate in more value-adding roles rather than performing repetitive and boring tasks that computers can undertake. Team members focusing on stimulating and high-value items also tend to create more innovative solutions to empower enterprise modernisation progress.

Remove Silos

Silos are proven to slow the whole enterprise modernisation life cycle, from architecting, designing, developing, marketing and selling products and services. A siloed culture can also impact the quality of the products due to a lack of integrated views. Enterprise departments in silos may not know each other's progress and cause some duplicate of works or rework. They may not produce a single integrated product or services to the consumers. Some departments in these traditional settings in the same organisations even compete with each other. Internal competition is an undesirable situation.

Agility approach requires moving from silos to a flatter structure to resolve the issues of isolated and hierarchical structures in large organisations. Enterprise Architects, following the agile method, must pay special attention to collaboration, co-locations, and face to face teamwork rather than having silos and hierarchies.

Enterprise Architects continuously need to deal with culture and modernising ecosystem implications. They must strive to break silos, instead of coming above, they create flat structures, resulting in collaborative self-managing teams with many domain experts as peers.

Manage your Backlog Effectively

Maintaining backlogs in agile methods is critical. Enterprise Architects make day to day management of backlogs in a priority order a habit. They manage their team's backlog for modernisation solutions effectively. Even if they perform the role of a scrum master or a product owner, these architects need to keep the team members accountable for their backlog items.

Since Enterprise Architects know the importance of prioritisation, they must continuously focus on the priority items and deal with the backlog items based on their priority orders. Their backlogs must run very efficiently and productively. Backlog management is a critical factor of modernisation sprints.

We need to set the priorities by using various considerations. One of the critical aspects is the creation of a minimum viable product using the Agile method. A Sprint is the shortest time bombed duration to create the minimum viable product. Consumer expectations, financial constraints, resource issues, and business priorities all have an impact on setting priorities for clearing backlogs.

Embrace Constant Change

Agile methods mandate change. Change management is a vital aspect of enterprise modernisation initiatives. Embracing change is critical to be successful in agile delivery. Adapting to constant change is very important for agility.

Managing every user story, clearing a backlog item and running a Sprint is all about constant change. Dealing with this constant change requires flexibility and agility in designing, developing and implementing agile solutions.

Enterprise Architects and their team members engaged in agile processes and solutions embrace the constant change. They become the change agents. Enterprise modernisation initiatives leading to the digital transformations certainly needs such a change-oriented agile approach.

Fail Fast

As we keep highlighting, one of the benefits of using agile methods come from the iterative approach. In other words, we tackle solutions in smaller chunks with agility. Agile methods enable the principles of the fail fast, fail early, fail cheaply. These notions are fundamental for successful modernisation goals.

Of course, we don't fail for the sake of failure. No one enjoys failure, but it is beneficial to fail earlier than later to keep the cost of failure low and be successful in the long run using the lessons learnt from smaller failures.

Even though it is called 'fail fast' it refers to constant trial and error leading to further intelligence and learning to deal with unknowns in a fast and effective way. Learnings from these trial and errors constitute the progress for designing, developing and implementing complex solutions for enterprise modernisation goals.

Cost and Revenue Relationship with Agility

In business, we can consider every resource and effort as a cost. Even though Enterprise Architects and other competent architects are well paid and costing business for their salaries, as they are cost-aware and know how to reduce cost with their capabilities, they make their projects profitable, generate more revenue, especially delivering with agility for modernisation. They focus on increasing efficiencies and lowering costs as part of their modernisation strategy.

Agile is a cost-focused and revenue-generating approach. Enterprise Architects can manage costs better and generate more revenue by adopting agile approaches in high impact tasks and solution development activities in modernisation solutions. Through incremental progress, prioritised backlog management, speedy iterative delivery through Sprints, Agile Enterprise Architects can prevent the cost of failure for big chunks of work items and more importantly they can turn the costs into revenues.

Agile Enterprise Architects responsible for enterprise modernisation initiatives are capable of turning costs to investment. With a strong vision, innovative approaches, and agile delivery capabilities, the costs incurred from the initiatives of these architects can be seen as an investment. Investment on visionary and well-performing Enterprise Architects can generate new businesses and bring substantial revenues in modernisation initiatives with their contributions both at tactical and strategic levels.

Chapter Summary and Key Points

Speed to market is one of the most fundamental requirements of businesses nowadays. Agile became the new norm in modernising enterprises. Products are expected to be released faster than they were in the past. Security updates and bug fixes are required more frequently.

There are many unknowns in the enterprise; hence, it is not possible to see the end product without constant trial and error in smaller scales for modernisation.

An agile approach allows the team members to test their ideas iteratively. If they fail, they fail quickly and cheaply without costing lots of funds to the initiatives.

Enterprise Architects must develop mental models on how technology users interact with their solution in each iteration. With their action-oriented approach, they must use the backlogs quickly and in priority orders.

Enterprise Architects must take a pragmatic approach to architecture development when engaged in modernisation programs. We know that predicting the future is very hard; therefore, creating an upfront paragon of architecture is not practical.

Enterprise Architects need to understand the value of automation. Applying automation to modernisation goals, we can reduce the number of resources required to maintain manual and tedious systems. Automation can address human errors and resolve potential errors quickly.

Enterprise Architects continuously need to deal with culture and modernising ecosystem implications. They must strive to break silos, instead of coming above, they create flat structures, resulting in collaborative self-managing teams with many domain experts as peers.

Even though it is called 'fail fast' it refers to constant trial and error leading to further intelligence and learning to deal with unknowns in a fast and effective way. Learnings from these trial and errors constitute the progress for designing, developing and implementing complex solutions for enterprise modernisation goals.

Agile Enterprise Architects responsible for enterprise modernisation initiatives are capable of turning costs to investment. With a strong vision, innovative approaches, and agile delivery capabilities, the costs incurred from the initiatives of these architects can be seen as an investment.

Chapter 8: Collaboration and Fusion for Modern Enterprise

Purpose

In this section, we have an overview of fusion and collaboration from a productivity angle in the modernising enterprise. Collaboration is essential to extend to fusion principles. Let's define these significant terms to reach a common understanding.

Once we establish a common understanding of productive collaboration and fusion principles consecutively, then we can explore how these characteristics help the Enterprise Architects excel in their modernisation goals, improve day to day duties, and make them contributing leaders. Now, let's start with the definition of collaboration.

Defining Collaboration

Collaboration may mean different things to different people. It is an overused term and loses its significance, especially with the emergence of internet technologies called collaborative tools, especially in a social media context.

In simple terms, we can define collaboration as a team of people working together for mutual goals. The team and mutual goals are essential entities of this simple framework. Our focus is of course, on the work aspect of the collaboration rather than entertainment or hobbies.

Collaboration may take place in different modes and formats. One example is two or more people sharing ideas for a project plan. At a basic level, people may also collaborate by writing using various documentation tools such as Box, Google docs, or network version of Microsoft Office products.

There are also emerging tools mainly used in mobile settings. These mobility tools are widespread in Agile methods. To give an idea, some of these tools are Slack, Trello, Twitter, Facebook Messenger, and many more.

Social media tools are touted as practical, useful, and highly valuable for collaboration purposes. However, when we carefully examine these tools, we can see that they are more information-sharing tools rather than actual collaboration tools. From my experience, the most productive and impactful collaboration tools are face to face meetings, telephone, and video conferencing.

Collaboration is an essential factor for Enterprise Architects to create outstanding results. These architects collaborate widely and productively. They also motivate their team members to collaborate effectively and efficiently by pointing out the common goals and making them compelling for collaboration.

Fusion for Enterprise Modernisation

Fusion is essential for enterprise modernisation. The term fusion refers to joining different things with different attributes or functions together to create a single new entity or form. The notion of fusion relates to concepts such as integration, blending, merging, amalgamation, and bonding. Fusion is closely related to collaboration from several angles. It is a type of collaboration designed for specific and advanced missions. Fusion principles suit the goals of enterprise modernisation.

Fusion principles aim to bring individuals from various backgrounds, small groups with different purposes, various teams with differing capabilities, communities of practices with different missions under a single umbrella for serving a joint mission. Fusion is the most advanced and effective type of collaboration especially required for complex and complicated modernisation initiatives with unique goals and market focus. Creating fusion-based collaboration can be very challenging. Enterprise Architects with extensive technical and people skills and experiences can create fusion-based collaboration.

Fusion can also refer to integrating old systems, tools, and processes and creating new systems. This transformative approach is a critical factor for enterprise modernisation goals. From an awareness perspective, Enterprise Architects need to understand the significance of fusion principles and apply them to help their organisations to modernise the enterprise effectively.

How to ignite and enable collaboration

There are different ways to enable collaboration. Enterprise Architects usually take responsibility to initiate collaboration. These architects must be passionate about their goals. They don't wait for collaboration to happen by itself. They know that nothing can happen by itself. Naturally, someone with leadership and architectural skills must initiate it. This action-oriented focus on collaboration is one of the outstanding characteristics of strategic Enterprise Architects, who are typically extrovert people.

Once Enterprise Architects initiate collaborative activities and invite their collaborators, then the process is maintained with necessary communication and engagement rules. Effective communication is a critical enabler of collaboration. Depending on the medium, both verbal and written communication types are essential for collaboration to happen.

Collaboration for co-located teams are usually conducted on face to face and can primarily be dynamic in delivery. However, geographically distant teams usually use video conferencing, telephone, chat programs, email or some agile collaboration tools. In remote teams, written communication is critical. Written communications can create some challenges, such as a careless piece of writing may cause some offence and kill the spirit of collaboration. Therefore, Enterprise Architects play an essential role in facilitating these types of communication by moderating communication channels delicately.

How to maintain collaboration

After Enterprise Architects initiate and enable collaboration, they need to maintain the desired outcomes. Enterprise Architects need to create the necessary process and procedures to maintain collaboration. Their leadership skills are necessary to achieve this goal in modernisation initiatives.

Even though they set the initial team and processes to support the team activities, it is also the responsibilities of other team members to contribute to the goals set by these collaborative plans. To this end, excellent leaders also take the role of motivators to keep the team inspired by showing their impactful vision and strategic goals.

By focusing on productive collaboration at various levels, Enterprise Architects leverage insights from cross-functional teams and community of practices to create differentiated value propositions for the modernisation goals.

Create a Magic of Collaboration

By undertaking many tasks to initiate and maintain collaboration, the strategic Enterprise Architects keep repeating these activities multiple times with multiple teams and integrate these teams to aggregate collaboration. The magic of collaboration starts with these repetitions. Successful repetitions make ripple effects for more success. In a relatively short time frame, these teams can create a collaborative culture aligned with the organisation's ecosystem and strategic goals.

This collaborative culture at work can be invaluable. When collaborative culture starts flourishing using fusion-based collaboration, a desirable phenomenon called innovation happens naturally. Collaboration and innovation are tightly coupled processes.

Innovation is one of the exciting results provided by a collaborative culture with diversity, inclusiveness and implementation of fusion approach. The power of connected people from diverse backgrounds for the same goal generates new ideas and insights. Some of these ideas and insights may touch people from different angles and further motivate them even to take more responsibilities in this ecosystem. With the ignition of the initial strategic technical leadership, this shift causes the emergence of new technical leaders in modernising enterprises. Innovation generates collaborative culture and can be highly desirable for creating new business and growing established businesses by modernising the enterprise leading to desired digital transformation goals.

This magical aspect of collaboration leading to innovation is an ideal situation for modernisation goals. Enterprise Architects must take advantage of this desirable situation by creating, maintaining, facilitating and further improving the situations.

Importance of influence for Collaboration

Influence is an essential strategic leadership attribute. It is particularly essential for collaboration. Enterprise Architects influence their collaborators with their responsibility, accountability, and demonstrated credibility.

Credibility in technical environments is critical. Enterprise Architects must be credible. These architects can earn the trust of their collaborators with credibility and integrity. Strategic Enterprise Architects must pay special attention to remain credible in their fields.

When we establish trust, another magic happens. People start sharing their true selves. They become more productive and more creative. A collaborative culture is an empowering contributor and enabler of modernising enterprises.

Importance of Diversity for Collaboration

Diversity is a critical factor in creating collaborative teams and inclusive cultures. Diversity is extra critical for modernisation due to the required creativity and innovation by people from different backgrounds, skills sets and experiences.

Trust is a requirement for diversity. Only with trust and trusted environments, people can show their true identities. When people start showing their true self, a diverse culture starts flourishing. Diversity is an enhancer of collaboration.

More importantly, with diversity, also innovation come to the picture. We can notice it stronger and faster. Diverse ideas ignite and accelerate innovation. With this approach, we can create new options and choices. Connecting those choices and options also make a ripple effect on the culture. With this understanding, we can conclude that diversity can be a valuable contributor to modernisation programs.

Chapter Summary and Key Points

Collaboration is an essential factor for Enterprise Architects to create outstanding results. These architects collaborate widely and productively. They also motivate their team members to collaborate effectively and efficiently by pointing out the common goals and making them compelling for collaboration.

The notion of fusion relates to concepts such as integration, blending, merging, amalgamation, and bonding. Fusion is closely related to collaboration from several angles. It is a type of collaboration designed for specific and advanced missions. Fusion principles suit the goals of enterprise modernisation.

Effective communication is a critical enabler of collaboration. Depending on the medium, both verbal and written communication types are essential for collaboration to happen.

By focusing on productive collaboration at various levels, Enterprise Architects leverage insights from cross-functional teams and community of practices to create differentiated value propositions for the modernisation goals.

This magical aspect of collaboration leading to innovation is an ideal situation for modernisation goals. Enterprise Architects must take advantage of this desirable situation by creating, maintaining, facilitating and further improving the situations.

Credibility in technical environments is critical. Enterprise Architects must be credible. These architects can earn the trust of their collaborators with credibility and integrity. Strategic Enterprise Architects must pay special attention to remain credible in their fields.

Trust is a requirement for diversity. Only with trust and trusted environments, people can show their true identities. When people start showing their true self, a diverse culture starts flourishing. Diversity is an enhancer of collaboration.

Chapter 9: Other Vital Technology Enablers for Modern Enterprise

Purpose

Enterprise Architects must possess a wide range of vital technical skills. There are many growing and emerging technologies that these technical leaders need to be conversant. These architects must focus on using emerging technologies as enablers of the modernisation goals.

The key technology enablers of enterprise modernisation are Cloud Computing, Mobile Technologies, IoT, Big Data, and Analytics. An integrated view of these technologies, associated processes and tools are critical. Besides, benchmarking of products and services are essential enablers of digital transformations.

In this section, we cover the prominent technologies and briefly introduce them by highlighting their importance for modernisation goals. This is not an exhaustive list. The focus is only on foundational technologies.

Let's touch on the critical technical skills that Enterprise Architects need to possess for leading successful modernisation initiatives.

Cloud Computing

Cloud computing became mainstream in organisations. Adaptation of Cloud computing became very rapid. We can use Cloud as a foundational enterprise modernisation tool. The cloud service model can expand or reduce computer resources based on service requirements. For example, Cloud can provide the maximum resources when we need a large amount of computing power or storage capacity for a specific task at a particular timeframe. Then we can release these resources after completing our specific mission. This elasticity and scalability provide value position for digital transformations.

'Pay per use' or 'pay as you go' is another essential characteristic that Cloud services model provides. The resources can be consumed based on the usage amount. Usage could be a short- or long-term basis. For example, consumers can pay based on computing power or storage amount they used. Related to 'pay per use', using 'on-demand' is another characteristic of the Cloud services model. Consumers can use when they demand the required services without upfront payment or dedicated investment for the IT resources in their organisation.

The recent commercial trend for using virtual machines in publicly available Cloud services are based on three types of instances such as on-demand instance, reserved instance and spot instance. In on-demand instance, there is no long-term commitment. Reserved instance is a relatively longer-term with a substantial discount compared to on-demand usage. The spot instance, the price is agreed based on bidding.

Cloud offers resiliency. This means that system failures such as servers or storage units can be automatically isolated with predefined instructions, and workloads are migrated to redundant virtual units without disrupting the service levels or consumer usage. Cloud's resilience attribute removes many of our supportability concerns in our solution requirements.

Based on consumer requirements, Cloud resources can be virtual or physical. This flexibility is created by multitenancy characteristic of the Cloud service model. For example, a Cloud service provider can host multiple user workloads in the same infrastructure without adversely affecting their privacy and security. If there are high-security requirements such as sensitive governmental services, isolation can be physical. We need to consider constraints and limitations which can affect the use of virtual services in multi-tenancy mode.

Flexible workload movement is another crucial attribute of Cloud service model. There may be times an organisation requires to run their workloads in a different time zone, and the workloads can easily be moved to a data centre in another country. This may be for several reasons such as reducing cost, providing a better service for a focus group in a different location or even regulatory requirements.

We will cover the details of Cloud Computing for enterprise modernisation in the next chapter.

IoT (Internet of Things)

IoT (Internet of Things) is another vital technology that Enterprise Architects need to understand. Substantial progress has been made in many disciplines owing to the use of IoT in creating new services and products. Some of these disciplines include environmental monitoring, manufacturing, infrastructure management, energy management, agriculture, healthcare, transportation, IT, electronics, material sciences and banking.

In the market, it is noticeable that IoT technologies are emerging and IoT solutions are growing exponentially. Some organisations estimate billions of devices in the next few years to connect to the global IoT ecosystem. The bottom line is that IoT is valuable for both business and economy, which is inevitable. From our current experience, we can construe that IoT will most likely have a substantial impact on our economy and the way we do business and commerce.

Consumers and service providers have an incredible interest and focus on this fantastic technology powered by the internet. The generation of new business for companies and new job roles that we cannot even name yet is imminent. Some believe that the IoT can be as important as the emergence of the internet itself. Some even point out that it can be the next big thing in our lives. These are, of course, speculations, combined with some media hype; however, time will tell as to whether the high expectations of IoT will be met. One key fact is that IoT is one of the primary enablers of the modernisation initiatives; hence, it is an essential skill that these Enterprise Architects need to possess. We also allocate a distinct chapter on this critical topic.

Big Data, Analytics & Machine Learning

Big Data and Data Analytics are beneficial technology domains that Enterprise Architects need to understand and use for creating insights and competitive advantage for their organisations.

Even though architecturally similar to traditional data, big data requires newer methods and tools to deal with data. The traditional methods and tools are not adequate to process big data. The process refers to capturing a substantial amount of data from multiple sources, storing analysing, searching, transferring, sharing, updating, visualising and governing huge volumes data such as petabytes or even exabytes.

Ironically, the main concern or aim of Big Data is not the amount of data but more advanced analytics techniques to produce value out of these large volumes of data. The advanced analytics in this context refers to approaches such as descriptive, predictive, prescriptive, and diagnostic analytics.

The descriptive analytics deals with situations such as what is happening right now based on incoming data. The predictive analytics refers to what might happen in the future. Prescriptive analytics deals with actions to be taken.

Diagnostic analytics ask the question of why something happened. Each analytics type serves difference scenarios and use-cases.

Big Data Analytics is a comprehensive business-driven discipline. At a high level, it aims to make quick business decisions, reduce the cost for a product or service, and test new market to create new products and services. Big Data analytics are used in all industries; the most commonly used industries are health care, life sciences, manufacturing, government, and retail.

We need new methods and tools to perform Big Data Analytics. There are emerging methods and many tools available on the market. Most of the methods are proprietary, but some are available via open-source programs. Some popular tools frequently mentioned in the Big Data Analytics publications are Aqua Data Studio, Azure HDinsight, IBM SPSS Modeler, Skytree, Talend, Splice Machine, Plotly, Lumify, Elasticsearch.

Besides, open-source has progressed well in this area and produced multiple powerful tools. Some commonly used open-source analytics tools are Apache Hadoop, Apache Spark, Apache Storm, Apache Cassandra, Apache SAMOA, Neo4j, MongoDB, and R programming environment. We cover the overview of these tools in the technology and tools section of this chapter.

Big Data analytics is a broad and growing area. We can better understand Big data analytics looking at its inherent characteristics. These characteristics can be summarised using 'C-terms' to remember easily. These terms are connection, conversion, cognition, configuration, content, customisation, cloud, cyber, and community. As these terms are self-explanatory, we don't go into details to explain each here.

Big Data analytics use various methods and techniques such as natural language processing, machine learning, data mining, association pattern mining, behavioural analytics, predictive analytics, descriptive analytics, prescriptive analytics, diagnostic analytics.

Machine Learning & Text Analytics

Machine learning refers to computer systems to learn and improve based on their learning from the analysis of large volumes of data sets without programming. It is part of the artificial intelligence domain in computer science. Due to its usefulness and impact, machine learning became a vital technology and tool for enterprise modernisation strategies leading to digital transformation.

Text analytics include computational linguistics, machine learning, and traditional statistical analysis. Text analytics focus on converting massive volumes of a machine or human-generated text into meaningful structures to create business insights and support decision-making.

There are various text analytics techniques. For example, IE (Information extraction) is one of the text analytics techniques which extract structured data from unstructured text. 'Text summarisation' is another technique which can automatically create a condensed summary of a document or selected groups of documents. This is especially useful for blogs, news, product documents, and scientific papers. NLP (Natural Language Processing) is another sophisticated text analytics technique interfaced as question and answers in natural language such as Siri in Apple products.

Cybersecurity

Cybersecurity is a necessary skill for Enterprise Architects working on modernisation initiatives. Cloud Computing, IoT and Big Data also mandate security at all levels. Broader security awareness and associated skills are essential for technical and technology leaders leading the modernisation and digital transformation initiatives.

Cybersecurity is a vast security domain and touches every aspect of security management, such as identity management, authentication, authorisation, and many more areas. Cybersecurity is a critical factor for successful modernisation and digital transformation solutions.

Related to advanced security, Blockchain, which is relatively new technology, is becoming critical for new security requirements which could be enablers for modernisation goals.

Network

The network is another essential skill that Enterprise Architects in modernisation initiatives must possess. Enterprise modernisation solutions touch every aspect of networking such as wide area, local area, wireless and many more networking types. They proliferate as far as Cloud, IoT and Big Data are concerned.

Since the network and associated communication technologies are the fundamental enablers of enterprise modernisation goals, understanding functions of network and network implications such as security, latency, bandwidth, are also important topics that technology leaders need to cover broadly and in-depth based on their involvement.

Mobility

Mobility is a critical interrelated technology domain in organisations hence Enterprise Architects need to understand and educate their teams for the effective use of mobility for innovations leading to business insights and collaboration across the organisation including the customers and partners.

The domain of Enterprise Mobile Management (EMM) includes essential components such as device management, application management, content management, email management, and unified endpoint management.

Mobility is associated with several architectural and business considerations such as network access, compliance, data management, workplace demographics, end-user accountability and BYOD (Bring Your Own Devices) concepts.

IT Service Management

IT service management covers an extensive array of technology, process, and tools. IT service management includes processes such as change management, problem management, incident management, service level management, capacity management, availability management, business continuity management, security management.

In addition, system management processes such as monitoring, alerting and event management can be covered under the umbrella term of IT Service Management. These processes are managed using many technological tools. More importantly, these tools need to be architected, integrated, designed and implemented coherently.

Understanding the dynamics of these tools within the context of modernisation initiatives are vital for successful outcomes. One of the best representations of IT Service model is implemented using popular ITIL (Information Technology Infrastructure Library.

Chapter Summary and Key Points

The key technology enablers of enterprise modernisation are Cloud Computing, Mobile Technologies, IoT, Big Data, and Analytics. An integrated view of these technologies, associated processes and tools are critical. Besides, benchmarking of products and services are essential enablers of digital transformations.

We can use Cloud as a foundational enterprise modernisation tool. The cloud service model can expand or reduce computer resources based on service requirements.

The bottom line is that IoT is valuable for both business and economy, which is inevitable. From our current experience, we can construe that IoT will most likely have a substantial impact on our economy and the way we do business and commerce. IoT is an enabler for enterprise modernisation.

Even though architecturally similar to traditional data, big data requires newer methods and tools to deal with data. Big Data analytics is a broad and growing area. We can better understand Big data analytics looking at its inherent characteristics.

Machine learning refers to computer systems to learn and improve based on their learning from the analysis of large volumes of data sets without programming. It is part of the artificial intelligence domain in computer science. Due to its usefulness and impact, machine learning became a vital technology and tool for enterprise modernisation strategies leading to digital transformation.

Text analytics include computational linguistics, machine learning, and traditional statistical analysis. Text analytics focus on converting massive volumes of a machine or human-generated text into meaningful structures to create business insights and support decision-making.

Cybersecurity is a necessary skill for Enterprise Architects working on modernisation initiatives. Cloud Computing, IoT and Big Data also mandate security at all levels. Broader security awareness and associated skills are essential for technical and technology leaders leading the modernisation and digital transformation initiatives.

Since the network and associated communication technologies are the fundamental enablers of enterprise modernisation goals, understanding functions of network and network implications such as security, latency, bandwidth, are also important topics that technology leaders need to cover broadly and in-depth based on their involvement.

Mobility is a critical interrelated technology domain in organisations hence Enterprise Architects need to understand and educate their teams for the effective use of mobility for innovations leading to business insights and collaboration across the organisation including the customers and partners.

IT service management covers an extensive array of technology, process, and tools. IT service management includes processes such as change management, problem management, incident management, service level management, capacity management, availability management, business continuity management, security management.

Chapter 10: Cloud Computing for Enterprise Modernisation

Importance of Cloud for Enterprise Modernisation

Cloud is a critical technology and service model for modern enterprises and workplaces. This technology is part of many modernisation and transformation programs globally. Almost every organisation has started their Cloud journey at least in the last 5 years. Every organisation I deal with or hear from colleagues, friends, or publications have some Cloud initiatives starting at the enterprise level. Cloud is a primary enabler of enterprise modernisation and transformation goals.

Cloud Service Model

The cloud service model can be a perfect fit to empower enterprise modernisation and transformation initiatives. The most desirable attributes of Cloud Computing are elasticity and scalability. The cloud service model can expand or reduce computer resources based on service requirements. For example, Cloud can provide the maximum resources when we need a large amount of computing power or storage capacity for a specific task at a particular timeframe. Then we can release these resources after completing our specific mission. This elasticity and scalability provide tremendous value position for enterprise far as the modernisation initiatives are concerned.

'Pay per use' or 'pay as you go' is another essential characteristic that Cloud services model provides. The resources can be consumed based on the usage amount. Usage could be a short- or long-term basis. For example, consumers can pay based on computing power or storage amount they used.

Pay-per-use and on-demand are other characteristics of the Cloud services model. Consumers can use when they demand the required services without upfront payment or dedicated investment for the IT resources in their organisation. The recent commercial trend for using virtual machines in publicly available Cloud services are based on three types of instances such as on-demand instance, reserved instance, and spot instance. In on-demand instance, there is no long-term commitment. Reserved instance is a relatively longer-term with a substantial discount compared to on-demand usage. The spot instance, the price is agreed based on bidding. For example, the AWS (Amazon Web Services) use this model in their Public Cloud service offerings.

Another characteristic that we are interested in our enterprise modernisation solutions is the resiliency that Cloud model offers. Predefined instructions in automated Cloud infrastructure can isolate the system failures and migrate the workloads to redundant units without disrupting the service level and consumer usage. This capability creates resiliency for the infrastructure. Resiliency is an essential requirement to modernise enterprise infrastructure.

Based on consumer requirements, we can allocate Cloud resources as virtual or physical. Multitenancy characteristic of the Cloud service model creates this useful flexibility. For example, a Cloud service provider can host multiple user workloads in the same infrastructure without adversely affecting their privacy and security requirements. If there are high-security requirements such as sensitive governmental services or corporate intellectual confidentiality, we can request a physical isolation model. We need to carefully consider constraints and limitations which can affect the use of virtual services in multi-tenancy mode.

Flexible workload movement is another crucial attribute of Cloud service model. There may be times an organisation requires to run their workloads in a different time zone. In this case we can quickly move the workloads to a data centre in another region or country. We can move workloads for several reasons such as reducing cost, providing a better service for a focus group in a different location or even regulatory requirements.

After reviewing these useful attributes of the Cloud services for enterprise modernisation initiatives, now let's touch on deployment models which can add further value to our modernisation and transformation goals.

Cloud Deployment Models for Modernisation

I want to keep this section concise as every architect nowadays knows about Cloud computing and the generic deployment models. Cloud training became a core requirement for the skill requirements of all type of architects. Enterprise Architects particularly pay substantial focus on Cloud deployment models in their organisations.

Our overview of Cloud deployment here is a contextual and not intended to be a general introduction. Our focus in this section is on the architectural considerations for enabling enterprise modernisation and transformation goals.

Cloud services offer three primary service models. The popular models are IaaS (Infrastructure as a Service), PaaS (Platform as a Service) and SaaS (Software as a Service). There are also several other service types, but instead of using their names, we collectively call them XaaS. This acronym covers any computing service that can be delivered via the internet and consumed pay as you go model without upfront purchase for their infrastructure or required licenses.

For enterprise modernisation programs, we may use IaaS, PaaS, and SaaS models based on our requirements.

Infrastructure, platforms and software cover a large chunk of enterprise IT systems. However, there is also the possibility that we can use other service types such as BPaaS (Business Process as a Service) and BDaaS (Big Data as a Service) models.

Another fundamental point that we need to know is the deployment model for Cloud. There are four types of deployment models for Cloud-based services. They are public, private, hybrid, and community.

Even though Public Cloud is the most commonly used by small, medium-sized businesses, start-up companies and individuals, we can also leverage it for enterprise-wide programs based on requirements. There are many Public Cloud services providers. The most well-known Public Cloud service providers are Amazon, Google, Microsoft, SalesForce, and Rackspace. These service providers have a wide range of offerings including infrastructure, platform, software and many other IT services.

Private Cloud is established privately by large organisations using Cloud technologies usually hosted on-premises or rented data centres. The primary purpose of a private Cloud is security and regulatory compliance. Our enterprise modernisation goals may require the deployment of Private Cloud in the enterprise. Let's keep in mind that this can be costly and time-consuming.

The third model is the Hybrid Cloud, which is an integrated combination of Private and Public Offerings. For example, an organisation can use Private Cloud for their particular workload which may require security and regulatory compliance. The same organisation can also subscribe to a Public Cloud for other purposes such as for their less mission-critical and generic workloads. For example, proof of concept, proof of technology, development, test, and pilot environments can be ideal candidates for Public Cloud subscription model. We can leverage the power of Public Cloud model for several aspects of the enterprise modernisation programs.

We also need to consider the Community Cloud deployment model. Organisations can use the Community Cloud model to collaborate and share their mutual projects on a common platform. Community Cloud model constitutes the connection of private Cloud access to two or more organisations' allocated partition of the Cloud services. We can deploy Community Clouds internally or externally to our enterprise.

For our enterprise modernisation initiatives, we need to consider these deployment models and choose the most appropriate model for our solutions. For example, if our solution holds sensitive data and cannot pass other geographies, then we need to consider Private Cloud services. If our workloads are not mission-critical and do not have any sensitive data, we can leverage the Public Cloud offerings.

Hybrid Cloud as Enterprise Focus

In this section, we cover what hybrid cloud means, what value propositions it presents, what financial benefits it brings to organisations. We also cover the significance of Hybrid Cloud for funding sponsors and delivery executives. There are vital considerations to be made for the Hybrid Cloud to be successful and profitable for enterprise modernisation purposes.

Hybrid Cloud includes a mix of on-premises and third-party service provision activities in an integrated and orchestrated manner. On-premise is usually known as a Private Cloud, and third-party service providers are known as Public Cloud. These integration and orchestration capabilities allow computing workloads to move between these two distinct (private and public) cloud models with desired optimal balance.

The Private Cloud on-premise is usually used to host security-sensitive and business-critical workloads. Whereas, the Public Cloud is extended to host generic and growing workloads, which are less security-sensitive and resource-intensive such as development or test environments.

In terms of key-value proposition and benefits, the Hybrid Cloud is a flexible model and provides better data and application deployment options. The primary use case for Hybrid Cloud is managing dynamic and unexpectedly spiking workloads, which require computation in real-time for customer demands in particular periods such as sales specials, holidays and other special events. As these times are perhaps once or twice a year, it is not productive for the enterprises to invest upfront hardware, software, licencing, management, and labour costs to create a computing environment which could be idle for nearly 90% of the time.

When up-time and resource constraints become concerns for an organisation, the primary workloads such as databases, applications, virtual desktops, mail servers and other hosting servers can be balanced optimally by extending the Private Cloud to Public Cloud. This particular demand-based solution model makes Hybrid Cloud appealing for the business owners, sponsors and the executives such as CEOs, CIOs or CTOs responsible for workload design, deployment, and support in agility.

As Hybrid Cloud deployment makes the Private Cloud more elastic and faster to grow on demand (pay as you go and utility-based consumption model) by extending to the Public Cloud, it creates almost limitless computing resources on-demand securely, including required performance and availability, based on SLAs (service level agreements).

This timely, agile and flexible solution, with no upfront payment, is one of the primary reasons why these C level funding executives and the delivery executives add the Hybrid Cloud to their portfolio as a priority item.

This business use case (optimally balanced workload, extended to public cloud) makes Hybrid Cloud model an area which rapidly develops and is embraced by industry and the service providers with millions of dollars of investment to fill a gap in this new demanding market.

The Hybrid Cloud truly matters to the C level executives who are responsible for the growth of their organisations because this model enables their organisations' economic model substantially move from CAPEX to OPEX model by meeting required performance, availability and security requirements and concerns.

As important as the above points, the ROI (Return on Investment) in extending to the Public Cloud is almost immediate. Therefore, this productive value proposition can be substantial for enterprise modernisation programs.

Now let's briefly touch the critical considerations in transforming Public Cloud to the Hybrid Cloud model. Like any modernisation project, the principal critical factor is rigorous planning. Yes, Public Cloud is ready to use and matter of subscribing the services on the Internet; however, the real challenge to extend the Private Cloud to the Public Cloud is the maintenance of internal workload balance and integration of multiple services. Creating this balance and integration may require a considerable amount of architectural and technical work.

Organisations need to assess their needs and plan to move incrementally due to the adverse impact of moving too fast and with too much stake at hand. For example, we need to consider non-functional requirements of all systems and applications including performance, security, availability (service level agreements), automation, orchestration, replication, and distribution mechanisms.

Selection of service providers is also essential. We need to determine whether they meet the organisation's critical needs, such as specific industry compliance requirements. Industry requirements may vary from industry to industry such as Banking, Telecommunication and Energy industries have different compliance requirements. Functionality and tools in Public Cloud offerings are also necessary. When we look at several top cloud service providers, we notice that each have different offerings and pricing models for different functions and the use of tools.

Hybrid Cloud can be a cost-effective model for organisations which have fluctuating workloads. Even though subscribing to a Public Model is more comfortable for an extension, to be able to maintain a balanced workload between Private and Public Cloud models, there is a need to plan, design and deploy intelligent workload management processes and load balancing technologies. Besides, internal organisational process, politics, skills and financial matters also need to be addressed and resolved before commencing the Public Cloud subscription services. Despite all, Hybrid Cloud is a winning approach and service model which many organisations have already commenced using it efficiently.

The primary consideration for adopting a Hybrid Cloud model to the enterprise modernisation program is to assess the readiness of the enterprise to move into this model. As Enterprise Architects, we need to lead the discussions, create awareness, add it to our enterprise modernisation roadmap, make some high-level cost comparisons, and inform our sponsoring executives.

Smart Cost Model

Cost is the number one factor in enterprise modernisation initiatives. In order to deal with this critical factor, Enterprise Architects need to develop smart cost models for creating Cloud roadmaps. A simple cost model can include a comparison of building your own Cloud versus subscribing to a Cloud service provider. Usually, subscribing to a Public Cloud is perceived to be more economical due to no upfront payment or some providers such as Google offering sustained usage discounts. However, there may be exceptions to this perception as each organisation has different capabilities and various factors affecting the profitability of using Public Cloud services.

I have seen some organisations using their existing hardware and software and leveraging their skilled employees can create a more economical Cloud system for enterprise modernisation purposes. Your smart cost model can validate the viability of this approach. Your smart cost model must include visible and invisible costs.

There may be many hidden costs both in building your own Cloud or subscribing to Public Cloud services. Some hidden costs that we identified during some assessments were the cost of patch management, system tuning, ongoing training, end-user device support, hardware and software refresh. Hidden costs are the most difficult ones to deal with in the enterprise modernisation programs. Therefore, we must be alert at all times.

Cloud Optimisation Activities

Cloud adoption in an enterprise may require several optimisation activities. One of the most important ones is the cost optimisation. We need to determine whether the current systems are providing value for delivering business.

Optimisation of many components such as compute power, storage, network, facilities, middleware, applications and data is critical. These optimisation considerations require some early decisions on whether to shift and lift, migrate, consolidate, or create a new environment. During this optimisation assessment, it can be useful to predict workloads based on several IOPS, storage volume size or CPUs. Cloud optimisation can be part of an enterprise modernisation assessment practice.

Workload Management

Workload planning and management is part of the enterprise modernisation programs. We can define the workload as the requests made by applications and their users. Workload management is critical for planning Cloud services in an enterprise.

Workload management refers to the location of executing data related to processing, storage, and analytics. There are different workloads. We need to categorise them to the appropriate groups. There can be two main types of workloads, static and dynamic. We can leverage Cloud microservices architecture to perform necessary assessments.

Once we categorise the workloads in the architectural and planning phase, we can make decisions on which workload to deploy in which Cloud service models. Then, these decisions go to the design and deployment phases in the enterprise modernisation lifecycle.

Cloud, Big Data and IoT Relationship

Cloud, Big Data and IoT are the foremost enablers of enterprise modernisation initiatives nowadays. IoT, Big Data and Cloud Computing are three distinct technology domains with overlapping use cases. Each technology has its own merits; however, the combination of three creates a synergy and the golden opportunity for businesses to reap the exponential benefits. This combination can create technological magic for innovation when adequately architected, designed, implemented and operated.

We can start with a high-level view of these technologies, defining them from architectural perspectives and provide an overview of their relationships in creating the synergies and potential benefits for business.

To identify the relationships amongst these three technologies, we can start with the IoT and Big Data relationship first. For enterprise modernisation, we can consider IoT as the input or source data for the Big Data solutions. Big Data includes many types of data sets; however, the IoT data is essential to create innovations, new insights, and new business opportunities.

Then, we need to understand where Cloud Computing fits in this magical combination. Cloud Computing presents enabling and empowering capabilities, not only as a hosting platform for the Big Data but also providing advanced processing and analytics in an economical, scalable, reliable and agile manner.

We can view IoT as an enriching factor for Big Data and Cloud services. With the contributions from the IoT and Cloud, the Big Data can achieve unprecedented results for creating new businesses and growing existing ones.

Big Data solutions without Cloud can be costly and complicated due to infrastructure requirements for storage, process and analytics requirements. Not only the enormous volume of the Big Data but also other vital characteristics such as a variety of data sources, velocity (speed), the veracity of data and required value from data in motion makes it a very complex system.

Of course, the scope of the Cloud is much bigger than just supporting the Big Data. However, we can look at Cloud Computing only as an enabler and empowering factor of the Big Data. When we are creating the Big Data architecture solutions for enterprise modernisation, it is critical to consider the integration of IoT and Cloud to our solutions. IoT provides real-time data from many sensors to the objects used in all industries nowadays. I offered the importance of IoT and several use cases for IoT in one of my books titled "A Practical Guide for IoT Solution Architects".

Cloud Quality and Adoption Considerations

From an architectural perspective, the quality of Cloud services for Big Data solutions have several characteristics. We need to consider several fundamental architectural points when we are architecting Big Data solution integrated with Cloud services model. We cannot just subscribe to a public Cloud service or only assume a private Cloud environment without performing comprehensive diligence.

We can develop a checklist for fundamental and desirable requirements. The following are some essential points to take into consideration. Let's beware that this is not an exhaustive list. It covers a few key points at a high level. However, these points may give you an idea of crucial points to consider.

As governance is a critical factor, we can start reviewing the governance structure. The solution needs to meet regulatory compliance requirements. For example, privacy is one of the key regulatory considerations.

By using the expertise of a security analyst or specialist, we need to look into all aspects of security, including authentication, identity management, authorisation, encryption, and many other aspects. Security is a fundamental systemic matter for Cloud solutions and services. One way of looking at it is whether you can trust the security of this specific Cloud solution or services to host your Big Data project. Business continuity and disaster recovery must be implemented, tested and validated. We need to check whether the cloud services we consider are independently audited.

All non-functional requirements such as performance, availability, scalability, interoperability, and so on need to be analysed, tracked and validated. We need to review service level agreements for these non-functional requirements; for example, how much uptime is guaranteed and what kind of performance levels are warranted.

We must articulate the cloud process and services in relevant documents accessible to the Big Data project teams and relevant data consumers. The usability of these documents is essential too.

Network connections and all other connectivity requirements must be verified and validated with the Cloud service providers. Fundamentally, no network, no Cloud! We may check what carriers are being used, what networking technologies and tools are used in the Cloud infrastructure. Big Data is entirely dependent on the network when the Cloud services are used for the solutions.

Applications, middleware components and other tools in the Cloud platform must be ready for use. From a Big Data solution perspective, we need to determine whether these applications, middleware tools, and other tools fit the purpose of our solution. In addition, these tools may require customisation, tuning and unique configurations. As Enterprise Architects, it is our responsibility to determine these requirements and ensure they are covered in the solution supportability.

System integration facilities, APIs also need to be made available in the Cloud hosting services. We need to check whether we can integrate our solutions based on available integration infrastructure and tools.

More importantly, as relevant to Big Data, the data management services and analytics tools need to be ready for use. Our subject matter experts need to verify the availability of these tools in the determined service agreement. As a good practice, starting to test the Cloud services with a small proof of concept to ensure it meets our Big Data solution requirements.

To start the Cloud adoption process for our Big Data solutions in modernisation programs, we need to create a comprehensive Cloud transition plan. This plan must cover every aspect of the adoption with multiple stakeholders in the organisation. It covers not only technical and architectural matters but also business, project, commercial and financial matters. Enterprise Architects can provide a high-level awareness and governance structure, but it is the solution architect's responsibility to ensure that the Cloud hosting environment is optimal to serve the Big Data solution.

To this end, we need to understand the quality of the services provided for the Cloud adoption and review the service level agreements to match our operational goals to host our Big Data solutions. An architectural requirements traceability and mapping the solution requirements with the provided service level can be a good practice to ensure the operability and serviceability of our Big Data solution.

After these rigorous architectural concerns for IoT, Big Data and Cloud combination, in the next chapter we further discuss the use of Big Data specifically for enterprise modernisation purposes.

Chapter Summary and Key Points

Cloud is a critical technology and service model for

modern enterprises and workplaces. This technology is part of many modernisation and transformation programs globally.

The cloud service model can be a perfect fit to empower enterprise modernisation and transformation initiatives. The most desirable attributes of Cloud Computing are elasticity and scalability.

Pay-per-use and on-demand are other characteristics of the Cloud services model. Consumers can use when they demand the required services without upfront payment or dedicated investment for the IT resources in their organisation.

Flexible workload movement is another crucial attribute of Cloud service model. There may be times an organisation requires to run their workloads in a different time zone. In this case we can quickly move the workloads to a data centre in another region or country.

Cloud services offer three primary service models. The popular models are IaaS (Infrastructure as a Service), PaaS (Platform as a Service) and SaaS (Software as a Service). There are also several other service types, but instead of using their names, we collectively call them XaaS.

Another fundamental point that we need to know is the deployment model for Cloud. There are four types of deployment models for Cloud-based services. They are public, private, hybrid, and community.

After Private and Public, the third model is the Hybrid Cloud, which is an integrated combination of Private and Public Offerings. For example, an organisation can use Private Cloud for their particular workload which may require security and regulatory compliance.

Cost is the number one factor in enterprise modernisation initiatives. In order to deal with this critical factor, Enterprise Architects need to develop smart cost models for creating Cloud roadmaps. A simple cost model can include a comparison of building your own Cloud versus subscribing to a Cloud service provider.

There may be many hidden costs both in building your own Cloud or subscribing to Public Cloud services. Some hidden costs that we identified during some assessments were the cost of patch management, system tuning, ongoing training, end-user device support, hardware and software refresh.

Optimisation of many components such as compute power, storage, network, facilities, middleware, applications and data is critical.

Once we categorise the workloads in the architectural and planning phase, we can make decisions on which workload to deploy in which Cloud service models. Then, these decisions go to the design and deployment phases in the enterprise modernisation lifecycle.

Cloud, Big Data and IoT are the foremost enablers of enterprise modernisation initiatives nowadays. IoT, Big Data and Cloud Computing are three distinct technology domains with overlapping use cases.

Business continuity and disaster recovery must be implemented, tested and validated. We need to check whether the cloud services we consider are independently audited.

System integration facilities, APIs also need to be made available in the Cloud hosting services. We need to check whether we can integrate our solutions based on available integration infrastructure and tools.

To start the Cloud adoption process for our Big Data solutions in modernisation programs, we need to create a comprehensive Cloud transition plan. This plan must cover every aspect of the adoption with multiple stakeholders.

Chapter 11: Big Data for Enterprise Modernisation

Purpose

One significant fact is that Big Data is ubiquitous in enterprises. Every enterprise generates massive amounts of data. Big data is different from traditional data. The main differences come from characteristics such as volume, velocity, variety, veracity, value and overall complexity of data sets in a data ecosystem.

There are many definitions of Big Data in the industry and academic publications however the most succinct yet comprehensive definition which I agree comes from the Gartner: "Big data is high-volume, high-velocity, and high-variety information assets that demand cost-effective, innovative forms of information processing for enhanced insight and decision making". The only missing keyword in this definition is the 'veracity'. I'd also add to this definition that these characteristics are interrelated and interdependent.

Volume refers to the size or amount of data sets. We can measure them in terabytes, petabytes or exabytes. There are no specific definitions to determine the threshold for Big Data volumes. Ironically, even though it is called the Big Data, and it is a signifier, the volume is not the main characteristics of the Big Data as far as architecture, design and deployments are concerned.

Velocity refers to the speed of producing data. Big Data sources generate high-speed data streams coming from real-time devices such as mobile phones, social media, IoT sensors, IoT edge gateways, and the Cloud data stores. Velocity is an essential factor in all phases of the Big Data architecture and management considerations.

Variety refers to multiple sources of data. The data sources include structured transactional data, semi-structured such as web sites or system logs, and unstructured data such as video, audio, animation, and pictures. Variety is also a significant factor for Big Data architecture and management considerations.

Veracity means the quality of the data. Since volume and velocity are enormous in Big Data, veracity is very challenging. It is essential to have quality output to make sense of data for business insights. Veracity is also related to value. Value is the primary purpose of Big Data to create new insights and gain business value from Big Data. We can create value with innovative and creative approaches taken by all the stakeholders of a Big Data solution. Overall complexity for Big Data refers to more data attributes and difficulty to extract desired value due to large volume, wide variety, enormous velocity and required veracity for the desired value.

Even though architecturally similar to traditional data, Big Data requires newer methods and tools to deal with data. The traditional methods and tools are not adequate to process Big Data. The process refers to capturing a substantial amount of data from multiple sources, storing analysing, searching, transferring, sharing, updating, visualising and governing huge volumes data in the magnitude of petabytes or even exabytes.

Ironically, the main concern or aim of Big Data is not the amount of data but more advanced analytics techniques to produce value out of these large volumes of data. The advanced analytics in this context refers to approaches such as descriptive, predictive, prescriptive, and diagnostic analytics.

The descriptive analytics deals with situations such as what is happening right now based on incoming data. The predictive analytics refers to what might happen in the future.

Prescriptive analytics deals with actions to be taken. Diagnostic analytics ask the question of why something happened. Each analytics type serves difference scenarios and use-cases.

For enterprise modernisation initiatives, we need to consider Big Data as a critical player in the ecosystem to create new insights and help to achieve the modernisation goals.

Big Data Lifecycle Management

Enterprise Architects need to understand the life cycle of Big Data for modernisation programs. Our roles and responsibilities may differ in different stages; however, we need to be on top of the life cycle management, especially from the governance perspective, end to end.

Based on my experience and input obtained from industry publications, from an architectural solutions perspective, a typical Big Data solution, similar to traditional data lifecycle, includes several distinct phases in the overall data lifecycle management.

Enterprise Architects are engaged in all phases of the lifecycle, providing different input for each stage. These phases may have different names in different data solution teams. Enterprise Architects must create a standard naming convention for the phases to bring everyone on the same page. Let's keep in mind that there is no rigorous universal systematic approach to the Big Data lifecycle as the discipline is still evolving. Names and approaches are continually changing based on ongoing experimentations. Let's familiarise with the phases that I propose to maintain common understanding and clarity.

Phase 1: Big Data Foundations

Phase 2: Big Data Acquisition

Phase 3: Big Data Preparation

Phase 4: Big Data Input

Phase 5: Big Data Processing

Phase 6: Big Data Output and Interpretation

Phase 7: Big Data Storage

Phase 8: Big Data Integration

Phase 9: Big Data Analytics

Phase 10: Big Data Consumption

Phase 11: Big Data Retention, Backup, and Archival

Phase 12: Big Data Destruction

Now, let's have an overview of each phase with guiding points. These are not official names. Therefore, we can customise these phases based on the data practices used in our organisation. Our enterprise architecture may have an ontology for the solution phases. In that case, we can use them.

Phase 1: Foundations: Foundation phase includes understanding and validating data requirements, solution scope, roles and responsibilities of stakeholders, data infrastructure preparation, technical and non-technical considerations, and understanding data rules in an organisation.

This phase requires a detailed plan facilitated ideally by a project manager with substantial input from the Big Data solution architects. A PDR (project definition report) must cover the non-technical matters such as project funding, commercials, and other issues. Enterprise Architects govern this phase.

Phase 2: Data Acquisition: This phase refers to collecting data. We can obtain data from various sources. These sources can be internal and external to the organisation.

Data sources can be structured forms such as transferred from a data warehouse, transaction systems, or semi-structured forms such as Web or system logs, or unstructured such as media files consist of videos, audios or pictures.

Enterprise Architects guide the Big Data architects in facilitating this phase optimally. Data governance, security, privacy, and quality controls start with the data collection phase. The lead Big Data solution architect needs to document the data collection strategy, requirements, architectural decisions, use cases, and technical specifications in this phase. Enterprise Architects review and approve the requirements and architectural decisions. Data and platform specialists review and approve the specifications.

Phase 3: Data Preparation: In the data preparation phase, we clean the collected raw data. We check the data rigorously for any inconsistencies, errors, and duplicates. We consistently remove any redundant, duplicated, incomplete and incorrect data sets and entries. This activity results in having a clean data set. Preparation of data is usually not an architectural task however Enterprise Architects need to govern this phase. They can delegate the details activities to the Big Data solution architects and specialists.

Phase 4: Data Input: Data input refers to sending data to planned target data repositories or systems. For example, we send the clean data to determined destinations such as CRM systems, data lakes, or data warehouse. In this phase, we transform the raw data into a useable format. Enterprise Architects govern this phase; however, delegate the activities to the Big Data architects and specialists.

Phase 5: Data Processing: Data Processing starts with processing the raw form of data. Then, we convert data into a readable format giving it the form and context. After this activity, we can interpret data by the selected data analytics tools. We can use generic or proprietary Big Data processing tools based on the data practices in our organisation. Some standard tools that we may consider are Hadoop MapReduce, Impala, Hive, Pig, and Spark SQL. The most common real-time data processing tool is HBase, and near real-time data processing tools is Spark Streaming. Data processing also includes activities such as data annotation, integration, aggregation, and representation.

In this phase, data may change its format based on requirements. We can use processed data in various data outputs such as in data lakes, for enterprise networks, and connected devices. We can further analyse data using advanced processing techniques and tools such as Spark MLib, Spark GraphX, and machine learning.

Data processing require various team members with different skills sets. While the lead solution architect leads the phase, data specialists, engineers and data scientists perform most of the activities. Enterprise Architects govern this phase from approach, process, technology and tool perspective.

Phase 6: Data Output and Interpretation: Data output is a phase where the data is in a format ready for consumption by the business users. We can transform data into useable formats such as plain text, graphs, processed images or video files. This phase announces the data ready for use and sends the data to the next stage for storing. This phase in some organisation is also called data ingestion aiming to export data for immediate use or future use and keep it in a database format. Ingestion process can be a real-time or batch format. Some standard Big Data ingestion tools are Sqoop, Flume, and Spark streaming.

Phase 7: Data Storage: Once we complete the data output phase, we store data in allocated storage units as pointed out by the data platform designs. Once data is stored, then it can be easily accessed by the defined user groups. Big

Data storage includes underlying technologies such as relational data storage or extended data storage such as HDFS and HBASE. We can consider the file formats text, binary, or another type of specialised formats such as Sequence, Avro and Parquet in data storage phase. Several architects and specialists participate in this phase. While Enterprise Architect set the standards, Infrastructure Architects build the platform with the input from the Big Data Architects.

Phase 8: Data Integration: Once the data is stored, in traditional models, it ends the process. However, for Big Data, there may be a need for the integration of stored data for various purposes. Some data models may require integration of data lakes with a data warehouse or data marts. There may also be application integration requirements. For example, some integration activities may comprise of integrating data with dashboards, tableau, websites, or data visualisations applications. This activity may overlap with the next phase, which is data analytics.

Phase 9: Data Analytics: Integrated data is ready for data analytics, which is the next phase. Data analytics is a significant component of Big Data. This phase is critical because we gain business value from Big Data. There can be a team responsible for data analytics led by a data scientist. Data architect has a limited role for this phase. Data architects need to ensure we complete this phase using architectural rigour for analytics. Enterprise Architects validate the standards.

Phase 10: Data Consumption: Once data analytics takes place, then we turn data into information ready for consumption by the internal or external users, including customers of the organisation.

Phase 11: Big Data Retention, Backup, and Archival: Some critical data may need to be backed up. There are data backup strategies, techniques, methods and tools that the

Enterprise and Solution architects need to identify, document, and obtain approval. We may need to archive some critical data for regulatory or other business reasons for a defined period. Enterprise Architects determine and document data retention strategy approved by the governing body in the data practice department.

Phase 12: Big Data Destruction: There may be regulatory requirements to destruct a particular type of data after a certain amount of times. These may change based on the industries that data belong. Even though there is a chronological order for the life cycle management, for producing Big Data solutions, some phases may slightly overlap; hence, we can perform them in parallel. The life cycle is the only guideline and can be customised based on the structure of the data solution team, data needs and dynamics of the owner organisation departments or the enterprise.

Big Data Solution Components

Big Data solution architecture begins with an understanding of the process end to end. We can classify the process under two broad categories. The first one is Data Management, and the second one is Data Analytics.

We need to understand data management activities such as data acquisition, extraction, cleansing, annotation, processing, integration, aggregation, and representation. Data Analytics components at a high level are activities such as modelling, analysis, interpretation, and visualisation.

In the subsequent sections, we cover several components to understand Big Data solutions. Key components to introduce are data types, principles, life-cycle management, platforms, quality specifications, governance, security, privacy analytics, semantics, patterns, data lakes, puddles, swamp, ponds and data warehouse. The following sections provide an overview of these components.

Big Data Platform

The first layer of the Big Data platform is the shared operational information zone consists of the data types such as data in motion, data at rest, and data in several other forms. It includes legacy data sources, new data sources, master data hubs, reference data hubs, and content repositories.

The second large layer is processing. This layer includes data ingestion, operational information, landing area, analytics zone, archive, real-time analytics, exploration, integrated warehouse, data mart zones. This layer needs to have a governance model for metadata catalogue including data security and disaster recovery of systems, storage and hosting and other infrastructure components such as Cloud.

The third layer is the analytics platform. It consists of real-time analytics, planning, forecasting, decision making, predictive analytics, data discovery, visualisations, dashboard, and other analytics features.

The fourth layer consists of outputs such as business processes, decision-making schemes, and point of interactions. Enterprise Architects need to govern this layer well. We need to provide access with established controls both for the data platform professionals such as data scientists, data architects, analytics experts, and business users. We need to engage a Security Architect or Specialist to analyse the requirements and take appropriate measures.

Level of the schema for the platform is a crucial architectural consideration. We can classify the level of schema under three categories, such as no schema, partially structured schema, and full structured schema. Control of schema is an enterprise concern; therefore, Enterprise Architects need to take control of this function.

To understand the type of schema, we can use examples. Some examples of no schema are video, audio and picture files; social media feed, partial schema such as email, instant messaging logs, system logs, call centre logs; and high schema can be structured sensor data and relational transaction data.

The data processing levels require architectural considerations. The processing levels could be raw data, validated data, transformed data and calculated data.

Another structural classification of data in this platform is related the business relevance. We can categorise the business relevance of data as external data, personal data, departmental data and enterprise data.

We need to define business vocabulary as a shared understanding of Big Data related to business analytics. Business vocabulary provides consistent terms to be used by the whole organisation. Business departments own business vocabulary. Enterprise Architects ensure that this is in place and adequately governed. Usually, business users maintain this vocabulary. This vocabulary describes the business content supported by the data models. More importantly, from an architectural perspective, this vocabulary can be a crucial input to the metadata catalogue hence, it can be an enterprise concern.

Big Data Governance

Data governance is a critical factor for Big Data solutions. The Big Data governance system needs to consider essential factors such as security, privacy, trust, operability, conformance, agility, innovation and transformation of data. It is also vital that at a fundamental level, a data governance infrastructure to be established and evolve for adoption at the enterprise level.

Governance may take consideration for different stakeholders in the ecosystem. For example, data architects are responsible for developing the governance of big data models; data scientist are accountable for analytics perspective. Business stakeholders are responsible for the governance of business models for producing business results for the data ecosystem in concern.

Big Data governance is a broad area and covers components, scope, requirements handling, strategy, architecture, design, development, analysis, tests, processing, components, relationships, input, output, business goals, insights, and all other aspects of data management and analytics. Enterprise Architects are responsible for end to end governance of Big Data architecture and the associated solutions.

Big Data Analytics

Big Data Analytics is a comprehensive business-driven discipline. At a high level, it aims to make quick business decisions, reduce the cost for a product or service, and test new market to create new products and services. We use Big Data analytics in all industries. The most commonly used industries are health care, life sciences, manufacturing, government, and retail.

We need methods and tools to perform Big Data Analytics. There are methods and many tools available on the market. As Big Data Analytics is relatively a new discipline, both methods and tools are still evolving. Most of the methods are proprietary; however, some are available via open-source programs. Some popular tools frequently mentioned in the Big Data Analytics publications are Aqua Data Studio, Azure HDinsight, IBM SPSS Modeler, Skytree, Talend, Splice Machine, Plotly, Lumify, Elasticsearch.

Open-source has progressed well in this area and

produced multiple powerful tools. Some commonly used open-source analytics tools are Apache Hadoop, Apache Spark, Apache Storm, Apache Cassandra, Apache SAMOA, Neo4j, MongoDB, and R programming environment. We cover the overview of these tools in the technology and tools section of this chapter.

Big Data analytics is a broad and growing area. We can better understand Big data analytics looking at its inherent characteristics. These characteristics can be summarised using nine 'C-terms' to remember easily. These terms are connection, conversion, cognition, configuration, content, customisation, cloud, cyber, and community. As these terms are self-explanatory, we don't go into details to explain each here. Many publications for data and information architecture cover these characteristics in detail. It can be useful for Enterprise Architects to understand them, especially for setting standards and maintaining governance.

Enterprise Architects also need to understand various methods and techniques used for Big Data Analytics. Most commonly used methods and techniques for Big Data Analytics are natural language processing, A/B testing (a.k.a. two-sample hypothesis testing), machine learning, data mining, association pattern mining, behavioural analytics, predictive analytics, descriptive analytics, prescriptive analytics, diagnostic analytics. We cover some of these techniques in the subsequent sections.

Type of Big Data Analytics

There are four significant types of Big Data analytics. They are descriptive, predictive, prescriptive, and diagnostic. Each type is different in scope and aims to answer different business questions and provide different insights. Let's briefly explain each.

Descriptive analytics covers the historical aspect of data to understand what happened in the past. It aims to interpret historical data and elicit conclusions from data analysis to gain business insights. Some of the common themes of descriptive analytics are sales growth, new customers, numbers of products sold and many other financial metrics to inform the sales and business executives.

Considering current and historical data, predictive analytics cover techniques that predict future outcomes. Predictive analytics look for patterns and capture relationships in data. For example, we can use linear regression techniques in machine learning and neural network to achieve the interdependencies of variables in captured data for predictive analytics. We can use it in many disciplines and various business purposes. Predicting customer purchase goals by analysing their shopping behaviour is an everyday use case for Big Data solutions.

Prescriptive analytics aims to find the best action for a given situation. This type of analysis looks for ways to determine the best outcome among various choices. Prescriptive analytics can be instrumental in mitigating risks, improve the accuracy of predictions, and take benefits of opportunities. This analytics type helps us analyse the interactions and potential decisions and provides the best solution.

Diagnostic analytics uses multiple techniques such as discovery, mining, correlations, comparing, and contrasting. Diagnostic analytics ask the question of why something has happened by examining the data and propose an answer to this fundamental question. It can be useful to find the root cause of situations.

Data Lakes, Ponds, Puddles and Swamps

For enterprise modernisation initiatives, we need to

understand new data platforms that can empower Big Data process and analytics. We touch on some key concepts and the relationships among them in this section.

Big Data architecture solutions require the use of the data lake model. Data lakes are fundamental and useful aspects of Big Data lifecycle management. We can define data lakes in the simplest terms as the dynamically clean and instantly useable data sources made available for specific purposes. The need for data lake comes from users to take advantage of clean data based on self-service approach without needing technical data professionals. Use of data lakes can be a critical business proposition for enterprise modernisation programs.

A data lake can be a single store of transformed enterprise data in the native format. They are usually well reported, visualised and analysed using advanced analytics. A data lake can include structured, semi-structured and unstructured data such as images, videos or sounds.

Data lakes are dynamic stores and can be fed iteratively as further clean data are discovered and transformed from multiple sources in the enterprise. For example, a data lake can store relational data from enterprise applications and non-relational data from IoT devices, social media, and mobile apps.

There are multiple use cases for data lakes. The most common ones are when real-time data analysis required for the data sources coming from various sources. Another use case can be related to the goals of having a complete view of customer data again coming from multiple sources. Auditing requirements and centralisation of data can also be use cases for data lakes. These use cases are relevant and can be significant for enterprise modernisation goals.

The business value of data lakes come from being able

to perform advanced analytics very quickly for data coming from various real-time sources such as clickstreams, social media, system logs. Use of data lakes helps the business stakeholders to identify opportunities rapidly, make informed decisions, and act on their decision expeditiously for speed to the market.

Data lakes can be implemented using various tools, techniques, and services. There are commercially available services as well as open-source services to establish data lakes. For example, commercial products such as Azure Data Lake, Amazon S3 and open source product Apache Hadoop file system are some data lake implementation enablers to consider for our solutions. There are many more tools and method to design, implement and execute data lake solutions.

Based on feedback obtained from many successful implementations of data lakes, it appears that an excellent choice of platform for data lakes is Hadoop. Hadoop, as an open-source system, is highly scalable, modular, technology agnostic, open-source, cost-effective and presents no schema limitations. Big Data and Storage solution architects embrace Hadoop. Enterprise Architects need to assess the suitability of Hadoop for their enterprise modernisation initiatives.

Designing data lakes require critical consideration of data types. For example, one key consideration is that if the purpose of data is unknown, it is better to keep data in raw format so that it can be used by data professionals in the future when it is needed.

One of the critical challenges of data lakes is security as the data comes to the lake in real-time from multiple uncontrolled sources. To address this challenge, a well-governing security architecture with access controls and semantic consistency need to be in place for the enterprise data lake. Data lake design is a specialist level activity usually conducted by an experienced storage architect or specialist.

Enterprise Architects need to set the standards and maintain the governance for the lifecycle of data lake initiatives.

In addition to data lakes, we also need to understand the data puddles and ponds. Data puddle is a tiny purpose-build data platform usually used by a specific single team mission in an organisation conducted by a marketing group or data scientist. They are also a right candidate for data-intensive ETL (Extract, Transform, Load) offloading engagements for a single team. Unlike data lakes, they are not data-driven processing allowing informed decisions at enterprise levels. Related to data puddles, another term used for a group of data puddles is data ponds. We can design data ponds for a small amount of data management purposes. One way of explaining a data pond is to resemble it to a data warehouse designed for Big Data processing. Enterprise Architects can provide input for choosing the right data deployment model with the help of Data and Information Architects.

Another important term related to data lakes that we need to understand is 'data swamp'. This term refers to an unmanaged data lake that may not be accessible by the intended consumers or may not provide desired business value. From lessons learned in the field, many unsuccessful implementations of data lakes, unfortunately, turned into data swamps. Data swamps are undesirable situations in an enterprise. Thus, Enterprise Architects need to consider these types of hard-learned lessons for data management strategy of the enterprise modernisation plans.

Big Data Architectural Considerations

Enterprise Architects create enterprise-wide custom solutions by understanding the use cases, requirements, the scope, and customer expectations. They leverage architectural skills, relevant technology, and tools to create these custom solutions. The custom solutions can be products or services depending on the goals and the scope of the projects.

Big Data solutions are distinct and require additional expertise. In addition to considering several architectural points, these solutions also require domain knowledge of data and information architecture. At the highest level, Enterprise Architects need to identify optimal approaches to collecting, storing, processing, analysing, and presenting Big Data. However, practical solutions are architected by Big Data or Information Architects.

Big Data solutions require heterogeneous technology and tools to fit the purpose. It is essential to realise that there is no single technology or tool which can provide all-purpose for developing Big Data solutions.

Besides, due to their dependencies and relationships to many components, attributes, and factors, Big Data solutions cannot be developed in isolation or silos. Enterprise Architects need to consider the entire ecosystem and break the silos in thinking and critical architectural factors that may affect the whole enterprise.

For Big Data solutions, we must focus on highly-scalable platforms, processes, technology, and tools. Due to its nature, scalability is a fundamental requirement for Big Data solutions. Compromising scalability, even in a small amount, can cause undesirable solutions, troubled projects, and failed service levels. Scalability is a critical factor for enterprise modernisation initiatives.

Modularity is another architectural consideration for Big Data solutions for enterprise modernisation goals. For modularity, we need to ensure the modules fits into the big picture. For example, the same data should be able to be used by different projects and technologies rather than creating unnecessary data access silos.

Taking data and database attributes into consideration, let's touch on some technical points here. We don't have to be a specialist in data management or database administration; however, we need to be aware of some architectural points. For example, Enterprise Architects may come across the terms ACID and CAP as frequently discussed data governance topics. They need to understand and guide the Big Data team for their implications at the enterprise level.

ACID (Atomicity, Consistency, Isolation, Durability) compliance is an essential guide to guarantee the validity of database transactions and sequence of operations when internal errors or system failures occur. However, ACID compliance may impact scalability.

CAP (Consistency, Availability, and Partition) is another architectural point to consider for distributed database systems. This proposition instructs that a trade-off must be made choosing one out of three. The reason is only two out of these three aspects are possible. You may check this from data reference publications to understand the implications in detail for your enterprise modernisation solutions.

Big Data architecture requires thinking out of the box and innovative ways of doing things. We need to understand the latest technologies and practices for Big Data solutions. For example, there is a trend in the industry for trying new methods of data analysis without binding to traditional EDW resources and ETL processes.

In terms of tools and technologies, we can consider mixing open source and commercial systems based on their applicability and meeting our requirements. For example, OLTP can be designed using commercially available relational databases for structured and open-source Casandra Database supporting semi-structured databases.

Data sources in the enterprise keep changing, and new sources are being available. In addition to legacy data sources, we need to consider new data sources in Big Data modernisation solutions. We need to determine the type of data sources required in our solutions.

From solution readiness and quality management perspectives, it is vital to determine the timelines of data ingestion in the enterprise. Data ingestion, as a critical aspect of Big Data in the modernisation context, is the process of importing, transferring, loading processing and storing data for use. It can be synchronous, or an asynchronous batched, or rea-time basis. We need to articulate these options with compelling reasons and obtain validating input and approvals from subject matter experts and the solution governance body.

We need to choose the type of processing to perform whether real-time or batch processing. Our data processing may involve descriptive, predictive, prescriptive, diagnostic, and ad-hoc. We also need to consider the latency expectation of processing. These factors can plan an important role in enterprise modernisation initiatives.

We need to determine how to access the data, for example, by random or sequential order. Besides, we need to consider data access patterns. Data access patterns are necessary to optimise data access requirements. There are many patterns available in data application integration and interface publications. For example, some common patterns are accelerating database resource initialisation, eliminating data access bottlenecks, and hiding obscure database semantics from data users.

Database optimisation is an essential architectural practice at the enterprise level. These techniques aim to improve the quality and speed for data access, read and write activities. Some of the critical considerations are using appropriate indexes, removing unnecessary indexes and minimising data transfers from client to server.

Sharding is another technique to consider. Sharding can be a necessary technique to consider with caution. Sharding is a kind of database partitioning. It splits large databased into smaller units. The primary use case for sharding is to isolate faults or address memory problems for the large data sets which become a bottleneck. As guidance, we need to use sharding as a last resort after trying all other optimisation methods as it can have several drawbacks such as back up problems, indexing issues, and even schema change difficulties. Usually Enterprise Architects do not go into details of sharding; however, they need to understand the concept and its implications to help the Big Data architecture team to make sound architectural decisions especially when a solution is presented in the modernisation Design Authority or Architecture Review Board meetings.

So far, we provided a very high-level view of architectural considerations at the enterprise level. These are the only tip of the iceberg in developing Big Data solutions. We don't go into the details of Big Data architecture as it is a domain level expertise rather than enterprise-level concern. Once we start the process and delve into requirements, we can come across many more considerations based on our industry, project goals and many other factors which some of them can be beyond our controls and may require domain expertise.

Therefore, it is essential to follow an established method, collaborative solution team, proven processes, leading technologies and well-supported tools to produce successful Big Data solutions. Enterprise Architects can guide the team with these critical foundational practices.

The next important point is the use of open-source tools in the enterprise. Use of open source tools can be very beneficial for enterprise modernisation programs. Let's briefly touch on the commonly used and recommended Big Data tool in the open-source space.

Overview of Open Source Big Data Tools

Open source is incredibly important and widespread for information technology hence equally crucial for Big Data and Analytics in the enterprise. It is a type licensing agreement which allows the developers and users to freely use the software, modify it, develop new ways to improve it and integrate to larger projects. It is a collaborative and innovative approach embraced by many IT organisations and consumer organisations. It is not only ideal for start-up companies and those companies with a tight IT budget but also enterprises struggling to have more flexible architectures for modernisation leading to digital transformations.

There are many open-source tools and technologies for Big Data and Analytics. In this section, we provide an overview of some essential and commonly used open-source tools to consider for the Big Data solutions. An awareness of these tools is fundamental for Enterprise Architects. Here's a summary of the famous open-source Big Data and Analytics tools.

Apache Hadoop is a platform for data storage and processing. Hadoop is scalable, fault-tolerant, flexible, cost-effective and open source. It is ideal for handling massive storage pools using the batch approach in distributed computing environments. We can use Hadoop for complex Big Data and Analytics solutions at the enterprise level.

Apache Cassandra is a semi-structured open source database. It is linearly scalable, high speed, and fault-tolerant. The principal use case for Cassandra is a transactional system requiring fast response and massive scalability. Cassandra is also widely used for Big Data and Analytics solutions at the enterprise level.

Apache Kafka is a stream processing software platform. Using Kafka, users can subscribe to commit logs and publish data to any number of systems or real-time applications. Kafka offers a unified, high-throughput, low-latency platform for real-time handling data feeds. Kafka platforms were initially developed by LinkedIn, used for a while, and donated to open source.

Apache Flume offers a simple and flexible architecture. The architecture of Flume is a reliable, distributed software for efficiently collecting, aggregating, and moving large amounts of log data in the Big Data ecosystem. We can use Flume for streaming data flows. Flume is fault-tolerant with many failover and recovery systems. Flume uses an extensible data model that allows for online analytic application.

Apache NiFi is an automation tool designed to automate the flow of data amongst the software components based on flow-based programming model. Currently, Cloudera supports for its commercial and development requirements. It has a portal for the users and uses TLS encryption for security.

Apache Samza is a near-real-time stream processing system. It provides an asynchronous framework for stream processing. Samza allows building stateful applications that process data in real-time from multiple sources. It is well known for offering fault tolerance, stateful processing, and isolation.

Apache Sqoop is a command-line interface application used to transfer data between Apache Hadoop and the relational databases. We can use it for incremental loads of a single table or free form SQL queries. We can use Sqoop with Hive and HBase to populate the tables.

Apache Chukwa is a system for data collection. Chukwa monitors large distributed systems and builds on the

MapReduce framework on HDFS (Hadoop Distributed File System). Chukwa is a scalable, flexible and robust system for data collection.

Apache Storm is a stream processing framework. The Storm is based on spouts and bolts to define data sources. It allows batch and distributed processing of streaming data. The Storm also enables real-time data processing.

Apache Spark is a framework that allows cluster computing for distributed environments. We can use Spark for general clustering needs. It provides fault tolerance and data parallelism. Spark's architectural foundation is based on resilient distributed dataset. The Dataframe API is an abstraction on top of the resilient distributed dataset. Spark has different editions, such as Core, SQL, Streaming, and GraphX.

Apache Hive is a data warehouse software. We can build Hive on Hadoop platform. Hive provides data query and supports the analysis of large datasets stored in HDFS. It offers a query language called HiveQL.

Apache HBase is a non-relational distributed database. HBase runs on top of HDFS. HBase provides Google's Bigtable-like capabilities for Hadoop. HBase is a fault-tolerant system.

MongoDB is a high performance, fault-tolerant, scalable, cross-platform and NoSQL database. It deals with unstructured data. It is developed by MongoDB Inc is licensed under the SSPL (Server-Side Public License), which is a kind of open-source product.

There are many more rapidly developing open-source software tools which can be used for various functions of data life cycle management in the enterprise. These tools can be very useful for enterprise modernisation programs focusing on Big Data and Analytics solutions. These tools are easily accessible and available based on open source licencing agreements.

Commercial Big Data and Analytics Tools

We can find many commercially available tools and technologies for Big Data and Analytics suitable to deploy across enterprise-wide solutions. These tools and technologies can be sold as products or services. An awareness of these products and services can be beneficial for Enterprise Architects.

Some of the most popular Big Data and Analytics platforms with associated tools are Google BigQuery, Hortonworks Data Platform, HP Bigdata, IBM Big Data, Microsoft Azure, SAP Bigdata Analytics, Teradata Bigdata Analytics, Amazon Web Services.

As coverage of these platforms and tools is comprehensive and exhaustive, it is beyond the scope of this book and deemed to be unnecessary to include them here.

Chapter Summary and Key Points

One significant fact is that Big Data is ubiquitous in enterprises. Every enterprise generates massive amounts of data. Big data is different from traditional data. The main differences come from characteristics such as volume, velocity, variety, veracity, value and overall complexity of data sets in a data ecosystem.

The descriptive analytics deals with situations such as what is happening right now based on incoming data. The predictive analytics refers to what might happen in the future. Prescriptive analytics deals with actions to be taken. Diagnostic analytics ask the question of why something happened. Each analytics type serves difference scenarios and use-cases.

We can classify the process under two broad categories. The first one is Data Management, and the second one is Data Analytics. We need to understand data management activities such as data acquisition, extraction, cleansing, annotation, processing, integration, aggregation, and representation. Data Analytics components at a high level are activities such as modelling, analysis, interpretation, and visualisation.

Data governance is a critical factor for Big Data solutions. The Big Data governance system needs to consider essential factors such as security, privacy, trust, operability, conformance, agility, innovation and transformation of data.

Big Data governance is a broad area and covers components, scope, requirements handling, strategy, architecture, design, development, analysis, tests, processing, components, relationships, input, output, business goals, insights, and all other aspects of data management and analytics. Enterprise Architects are responsible for end to end governance of Big Data architecture and the associated solutions.

Most of the methods are proprietary; however, some are available via open-source programs. Some popular tools frequently mentioned in the Big Data Analytics publications are Aqua Data Studio, Azure HDinsight, IBM SPSS Modeler, Skytree, Talend, Splice Machine, Plotly, Lumify, Elasticsearch.

Some commonly used open-source analytics tools are Apache Hadoop, Apache Spark, Apache Storm, Apache Cassandra, Apache SAMOA, Neo4j, MongoDB, and R programming environment.

Enterprise Architects also need to understand various methods and techniques used for Big Data Analytics. Most commonly used methods and techniques for Big Data Analytics are natural language processing, two-sample hypothesis testing, machine learning, data mining, association pattern mining, behavioural analytics, predictive analytics, descriptive analytics, prescriptive analytics, diagnostic analytics.

Big Data architecture solutions require the use of the data lake model. Data lakes are fundamental and useful aspects of Big Data lifecycle management. A data lake can be a single store of transformed enterprise data in the native format.

The business value of data lakes come from being able to perform advanced analytics very quickly for data coming from various real-time sources such as clickstreams, social media, system logs.

Big Data solutions require heterogeneous technology and tools to fit the purpose. It is essential to realise that there is no single technology or tool which can provide all-purpose for developing Big Data solutions.

Modularity is another architectural consideration for Big Data solutions for enterprise modernisation goals. For modularity, we need to ensure the modules fits into the big picture. For example, the same data should be able to be used by different projects and technologies rather than creating unnecessary data access silos.

ACID (Atomicity, Consistency, Isolation, Durability) compliance is an essential guide to guarantee the validity of database transactions and sequence of operations when internal errors or system failures occur.

CAP (Consistency, Availability, and Partition) is another architectural point to consider for distributed database systems. This proposition instructs that a trade-off must be made choosing one out of three.

We need to choose the type of processing to perform

whether real-time or batch processing. Our data processing may involve descriptive, predictive, prescriptive, diagnostic, and ad-hoc.

Data access patterns are necessary to optimise data access requirements. There are many patterns available in data application integration and interface publications. For example, some common patterns are accelerating database resource initialisation, eliminating data access bottlenecks, and hiding obscure database semantics from data users.

There are many open-source tools and technologies for Big Data and Analytics such as Hadoop, Kafka, Flume, Sqoop, and Cassandra. An awareness of these tools is fundamental for Enterprise Architects.

Some of the most popular Big Data and Analytics platforms with associated tools are Google BigQuery, Hortonworks Data Platform, HP Bigdata, IBM Big Data, Microsoft Azure, SAP Bigdata Analytics, Teradata Bigdata Analytics, Amazon Web Services.

Chapter 12: IoT for Enterprise Modernisation

IoT Value Propositions

The main benefit and value proposition of IoT comes from collecting an enormous amount of data from various means and devices in the enterprise and then building services based on analyses of these massive amounts of data. Developing new services from such a collection of data would result in a substantial outcome with multiple architectural and business implications.

Business embrace IoT because it helps us predict the future; hence, the more data provided by the IoT systems, the better the analyses and outcomes can be. These data-rich analyses help us predict the future better and intervene before any potential damage occurs.

As IoT synthesises data via cognitive analytics, IoT solutions can help us gain better insights from structured, semi-structured, unstructured, dynamic or static data by integrating with cognitive systems. Like humans, a cognitive system undertakes the duties of learning, understanding, planning, problem-solving, deciding, analysing, synthesising and assessing.

We can use IoT solutions in many facets of the enterprise. These solutions can be used for departments solutions, enterprise-wide, and external entities to the enterprise to predict what we need and want.

For enterprise modernisation purposes, as an extended electronic ecosystem, IoT solutions can help to eliminate cumbersome technology affecting the performance of the organisations.

IoT can offer several applications at large scale for enterprises serving different industries. Some typical applications of IoT solutions are industrial control, robotics, medical, workplace safety, and security, embedded sensing in buildings, remote control, traffic control and most recently self-driving cars.

Architectural Implications of Massive IoT Data for Enterprise Modernisation

From an architectural perspective, we need to be aware the IoT devices generate massive amounts of data on an ongoing basis. These data sets go to the full data management life cycle; for example, in storing, analysing, re-building, and archiving. We must carefully consider the amount of data produced by IoT devices. The voluminous data in the enterprise require careful performance, scalability and availability measures.

When dealing with IoT in the modernisation programs, Enterprise Architects must take the responsibility of data management requirements at the enterprise level. We need to simulate the actual workload models based on the functional and non-functional requirements. We also need to consider historical data and future growth as part of the requirements analysis for performance.

Due to potential implications for enterprise, we must plan data collection via IoT sensors carefully. First, we need to determine the type of physical signals to measure. Then, we need to identify the number of sensors to be used and the speed of signals for these sensors in our data acquisition plan. Enterprise Architects need to closely work with the IoT Solution Architects to create stringent governance around data collection plans.

In addition to the challenges of massive data, application usage patterns are also an essential factor for the performance of IoT solutions in the enterprise modernisation initiatives. In particular, the processors and memory of the servers hosting the IoT applications need to be considered carefully using benchmarks.

Using benchmarks for application, data, and infrastructure, we need to create an exclusive IoT performance model and a set of test strategies for modernisation solutions. The IoT performance model mandates more data storage capacity, faster processes, more memory, and faster network infrastructure. While in the traditional performance models, we mainly consider user simulations, in the IoT Performance models, we also consider the simulation of devices, sensors, and actuators across the enterprise.

From a data management perspective, it is paramount to be aware of data frequency shared amongst devices. We need to consider not only the amount of data produced and processed but also accessed and shared frequently by multiple entities of the IoT ecosystem.

We must be mindful that the monitoring of these devices also creates a tremendous amount of data. If we always add the alerts and other system management functions to keep these devices well-performing and available, we need to have a comprehensive performance model, including the system and service management of the complex IoT ecosystem. IoT solutions for modernisations span across data, security, application and integration architectures.

IoT Cloud for Enterprise Modernisation

We the importance and the recent trends for Cloud Computing in previous chapters. Let's keep in mind that Cloud marked a paradigm shift to Information Technology and Computing field. IoT Cloud is a critical player in the ecosystem to enable enterprise modernisation capabilities. The central role the Cloud plays in IoT is to facilitate the data integration of the solution components for modernisation goals.

IoT solutions are mainly used to provide real-time information to consumers. The data required to generate real-time data can be massive in scale. The Cloud, along with computing power, storage, analytics, metering, and billing components, can make this information available for the consumers effectively.

One of the business value propositions of IoT for enterprise modernisation is the integration of Cloud to IoT, which can create new revenue streams for the organisation. Integrating the Cloud with the IoT can create new business models enriched by real-time analysis and directly-consumed information at the same time. In other words, without the Cloud, the IoT can hardly add any value due to its real-time data and information-rich nature.

The addition of the Cloud to the IoT can also contribute to improved security, availability and performance of the IoT solutions in the modernising enterprise. If we use a Public Cloud offering, let's keep in mind that Cloud providers have rigorous security, availability and performance metrics established based on a service consumption model. In particular, IoT-enabled Cloud systems seem to pose additional security measures.

Another architectural consideration is the use of Edge computing. When integrated with Edge computing, Cloud computing can add better value to the IoT ecosystem. The main reason for this is that Edge computing can do the filtering for the Cloud to focus on the usable data.

Enterprise Architects need to understand Cloud Computing architecture and how to integrate it into IoT solutions at the enterprise level. Being aware of the capabilities of Cloud technologies can be beneficial in creating large-scale commercial IoT solutions for enterprise modernisation initiatives.

Implications of IoT Analytics Computation

IoT solutions need computers to perform analytics and intelligence activities. Such tasks are hosted by Cloud platforms, such as analytics applications in which computation performance is essential. We also need to consider the implication of massive data for storage platform performance. For analytics storage, we need to make an architectural decision as to whether local storage or cloud-based storage can suit our requirements. This architectural decision is necessary to address cost and performance concerns at the enterprise level.

We can consider using IoT Analytics as a consumption-based service for cost-effectiveness. For example, AWS IoT Analytics is a fully-managed IoT analytics service that collects, pre-processes, enriches, stores and analyses IoT device data. AWS customers can also bring their custom analysis packaged in a container to execute AWS IoT Analytics. This Public Cloud offering can be beneficial to deal with the cost of the solutions for enterprise modernisation.

Enterprise Architects also need to focus on the representation of data available to enterprise consumers in visually compelling formats. For example, enterprise consumers can use analytics to make sense of data, such as key performance indicators in the visualisation application in dashboards. These dashboards can include risk management views, errors, bottlenecks and view the Internet of Things in real-time.

Considering Data Lakes for Enterprise IoT

We covered the data lakes in previous chapters. Let's

be mindful that IoT introduces new ways to collect data from various real-time data sources coming from the sensors of connected devices such as smart products, vehicles, and many other devices across the enterprise. Using a data lake for IoT generated rich data makes it easier to store and perform analytics for IoT data. The speed of using clean data (aggregated in a single place) for analytics can help discover ways to reduce operational costs and increase the quality of data. To this end, we need to aggregate IoT data sets in a single centralised place like data lakes.

IoT Architectural Challenges for Enterprise

There are several challenges related to IoT solutions in the enterprise. The challenges are multiple angles, such as architectural, technical, and non-technical. The most common architectural challenges for IoT are mobility, scalability, capacity, extendibility, interoperability, network bottlenecks, and connectivity.

Mobility is a common IoT Architecture Non-Functional aspect affecting the solutions across the enterprise. IoT devices need to move a lot and change their IP address and networks frequently based on their locations. For example, the routing protocols, such as RPL, must reconstruct the DODAG (Destination Oriented, Directed Acyclic Graph) each time a node goes off the network or joins the network, which adds substantial overhead. These granular technical details, which concern mobility, may have a severe impact on solution performance, availability, security, and cost in the enterprise.

IoT Solutions require overall scalability and capacity plans. IoT applications integrate with and serve multiple devices in the ecosystem. Managing the distribution of devices across networks and the enterprise application landscape can be complicated. We may need a dynamic increase or decrease in capacity, coupled with vertical and horizontal scalability and extendibility of the solutions in the enterprise. IoT applications need to be tolerant of new services and devices joining the network at a fast speed. Addressing this challenge requires dynamic scalability and enormous extendibility.

Interoperability means that heterogeneous devices, solution components, elements, and protocols need to be able to work with each other harmoniously. Maintaining the interoperability in an IoT ecosystem is another challenge owing to the wealth of platforms, solution components, devices and protocols used in IoT ecosystems.

Network bottlenecks adversely affect availability, performance and the cost of products or services in productions, making the service level agreements challenging to meet. Apart from latency related to the distance, several other factors are causing the network bottlenecks. Some common causes of network bottlenecks are malfunctioning devices, having an excessive number of devices connected to the networks, limited bandwidth, and overcapacity for server utilisation.

Several considerations also need to be made when it comes to internet connectivity; for example, the type of Internet services, internet service providers, usage cost, communication speed. Let's remember from the mobility section that mobile devices, such as moving vehicles, require unique internet connections, such as multi-service providers based on their current locations. For example, a device moving in Europe may require internet connectivity from a French Internet Service Provider when it is in France and from a German Internet Service Provider when it is in Germany.

IoT Security and Privacy Concerns

The major IoT concerns revolve around security and

privacy for the enterprise. IoT technologies are rapidly-changing, expanding and transforming to different functions and shapes; hence, IoT technologies can have a tremendous impact on security. The previous security solutions may not meet newer solutions for the enterprise. We need fresh security approaches to address new risks, issues, and dependencies. A recent addition to IoT security is the integration of blockchain to create secure and reliable connections. Blockchain enables the smart IoT devices to control, monitor and automate using the secure and reliable approach. Consideration of Blockchain for the enterprise modernisation initiatives may be beneficial to address security and privacy concerns.

Privacy is related to security. It is well-known that security risks can cause privacy issues. IoT privacy concerns are complex and complicated due to their nature; that is, they vary from country to country and are not always overt or obvious. Therefore, to begin with, Enterprise Architects need to pay special attention to privacy requirements at the enterprise level. Then, applying architectural rigours, such as adding privacy concerns to the architectural assessment and applying stringent risk management and mitigation process, can be very useful.

Chapter Summary and Key Points

The main benefit and value proposition of IoT comes from collecting an enormous amount of data from various means and devices in the enterprise and then building services based on analyses of these massive amounts of data.

As IoT synthesises data via cognitive analytics, IoT solutions can help us gain better insights from structured, semi-structured, unstructured, dynamic or static data by integrating with cognitive systems.

From an architectural perspective, we need to be aware

the IoT devices generate massive amounts of data on an ongoing basis. These data sets go to the full data management life cycle; for example, in storing, analysing, re-building, and archiving.

Due to potential implications for enterprise, we must plan data collection via IoT sensors carefully. First, we need to determine the type of physical signals to measure. Then, we need to identify the number of sensors to be used and the speed of signals for these sensors in our data acquisition plan.

Using benchmarks for application, data, and infrastructure, we need to create an exclusive IoT performance model and a set of test strategies for modernisation solutions.

We must be mindful that the monitoring of these devices also creates a tremendous amount of data. If we always add the alerts and other system management functions to keep these devices well-performing and available, we need to have a comprehensive performance model.

One of the business value propositions of IoT for enterprise modernisation is the integration of Cloud to IoT, which can create new revenue streams for the organisation.

Another architectural consideration is the use of Edge computing. When integrated with Edge computing, Cloud computing can add better value to the IoT ecosystem. The main reason for this is that Edge computing can do the filtering for the Cloud to focus on the usable data.

Enterprise Architects also need to focus on the representation of data available to enterprise consumers in visually compelling formats.

IoT Solutions require overall scalability and capacity plans. IoT applications integrate with and serve multiple devices in the ecosystem.

Maintaining the interoperability in an IoT ecosystem is another challenge owing to the wealth of platforms, solution components, devices and protocols used in IoT ecosystems.

Network bottlenecks adversely affect availability, performance and the cost of products or services in productions, making the service level agreements challenging to meet.

Several considerations also need to be made when it comes to internet connectivity; for example, the type of Internet services, internet service providers, usage cost, communication speed.

The major IoT concerns revolve around security and privacy for the enterprise.

Privacy is related to security. It is well-known that security risks can cause privacy issues. IoT privacy concerns are complex and complicated due to their nature.

Chapter 13: Enterprise Mobility

Enterprise Mobility Definition

Enterprise mobility is a critical aspect of modernisation. Mobility involves people, process, technology and tools at a massive scale. Mobility is essential for people in the enterprise. The demand for mobility is rapidly increasing. The process for mobility is also challenged to meet the demands of consumers. Technology and tools are proliferating. Mobile devices, mobile phones, mobile computers, tablets, wireless networks are a few to mention.

Mobility Device Management

Lifecycle management for mobile devices is an essential architectural consideration in enterprise modernisation initiatives. Managing mobile devices can be daunting from many angles. The life cycle for mobile devices can be much shorter than traditional computing and telecommunication devices.

Another architectural challenge related to mobile devices is dealing with quantity. In the past there were only office phones and people used to share them. Nowadays, workers have multiple mobile phones. Having multiple mobile devices per person may equate to thousands of mobile devices to consider at the enterprise level.

In addition to quantity, the user in the enterprise may change the mobile devices frequently. These frequent changes require consideration of applications and software updates for these devices.

Enterprise modernisation strategies must consider the challenges associated with these mobile devices. Enterprise

Architects need to create dynamic and flexible governance to address the concerns related to the use and lifecycle management of these devices.

Enterprise Security Implications for Mobility

The security implications of mobile devices are massive challenges. They create many security vulnerabilities for enterprises. Software updates can be persistent and very frequent. Frequent updates and patching can create a massive workload for the IT support departments.

Use of these mobile devices increases information consumption in the enterprise dramatically. Security control of the data can be daunting too. These security implications cross the data and application domains; hence, a collaborative effort among the Security, Data and Application Architects are required. Enterprise Architects must coordinate this collaboration across other architectural domains in the enterprise.

These critical challenges created by mobile devices are real and evident in the enterprise. Therefore, enterprise modernisation initiative must consider these challenges and find practical and innovative ways to address them.

Mobile Business Intelligence

Mobile business intelligence, also known as Mobile BI is an essential requirement for enterprises to stay competitive, open new markets, and create new revenue streams. Mobile BI includes both real-time and historical information for analysing mobile devices such as phones and tablets. The primary purpose of Mobile BI is to provide insights, based on past and current information, for business decision making.

Mobile BI is necessary for the overall support of mobile devices in the enterprise ecosystem. This intelligence, providing a broad perspective on the business data, sales figures, consumption figures and performance statistics, can be valuable for enterprise modernisation. By using the analytics on mobile progress in an enterprise can be very useful to develop a new business model and improve the current models.

Product and service providers widely use Mobile BI. Some established and popular Mobile BI environments are publicly accessible services such as Appstore by Apple, Google Play Store, and Samsung Galaxy Store. Enterprise modernisation programs can model these well-functioning services to create and improve their current Mobile BI strategy, service models, and offerings.

Unified Endpoint Management

A unified endpoint management practice is essential for enterprise modernisation initiatives. This includes relevant software tools and centralised management interfaces for consumers. This centralisation is necessary to improve the security capabilities and also allow a collaborative content sharing for the consumers and other stakeholders. We need to integrate unified endpoint management to our enterprise modernisation program structure.

Importance of Mobility for Enterprise Modernisation

Mobility is an inevitable part of our lives at home and in the workplace. Fortunately, or unfortunately, it created a bridge between homes and workplaces. In some ways employers can easily access their employees; however, the privacy of employees are affected by this easy accessibility.

The reality is that we cannot do business without the use of mobile devices any more. Mobility is an essential part of the enterprise. It touches every aspect of the enterprise. We cannot have a digital workplace without proper mobility architecture in place. We cannot have a modern enterprise without including the mobility to the equation. Due to these compelling reasons, we must approach mobility from strategic and architectural perspectives to properly integrate it into the culture and ecosystem of the modernising enterprise.

Chapter Summary and Key Points

Enterprise mobility is a critical aspect of modernisation. Mobility involves people, process, technology and tools at a massive scale.

Lifecycle management for mobile devices is an essential architectural consideration in enterprise modernisation initiatives. Managing mobile devices can be daunting from many angles.

In addition to quantity, the user in the enterprise may change the mobile devices frequently. These frequent changes require consideration of applications and software updates for these devices.

The security implications of mobile devices are massive challenges. They create many security vulnerabilities for enterprises. Software updates can be persistent and very frequent.

Mobile business intelligence, also known as Mobile BI is an essential requirement for enterprises to stay competitive, open new markets, and create new revenue streams.

Some established and popular Mobile BI environments are publicly accessible services such as Appstore by Apple, Google Play Store, and Samsung Galaxy Store.

Enterprise modernisation programs can model these well-functioning services to create and improve their current Mobile BI strategy, service models, and offerings.

Chapter 14: Conclusions

Covering significant aspects of enterprise modernisation from architectural perspectives in the previous 11 chapters, we reached to the final chapter. In this concluding chapter, we provide a review of the critical points. My aim for this chapter is to highlight significant points so that you can reinforce your learning from the previous chapters.

We started discussing enterprise architecture at a high level. The Enterprise Architecture discipline in Information Technology defines a macro level IT architecture at the enterprise level focusing on the mapping of IT capabilities to business needs using a structured governance method.

The focus of EA is broad and covers defining and describing the relationships, logical flows, implementation of business processes, activities, functions, data, information, applications, underlying technology, and supportive tools in the enterprise.

EA has five distinct phases. The phases in order of maturity are initial, baseline, target, integrated, and optimised. Enterprise modernisation initiatives must consider these phases and deal with them both individually and in an integrated manner.

The most common models are the Business Reference Model, the Components Reference Model, the Technical Reference Model, the Data Reference Model, and the Performance Reference Model.

Enterprise modernisation requires substantial simplification approach. The most common simplification technique for enterprise architecture is the partitioning approach. Another way of simplifying a system is reducing the quantity. After partitioning and simplifying the third critical method is iterating.

Everything in enterprise transformation generates substantial cost. There are known and hidden costs. It is relatively more comfortable to deal with the known costs; however, the challenge is to deal with the hidden costs.

Enterprise Architects need to pay attention to the SLAs from the early stages of the modernisation solution life cycle. The higher the quality of the solutions, the easier it is for SLAs to meet when the solutions are in production and the operational state.

Enterprise modernisation is a long journey moving the enterprise from chaos to coherence. Both a top-down and bottom-up approach can be applied. At the top tier business, IT processes and at the bottom tier IT infrastructure.

By using the strategy and considering the dependencies Enterprise Architects develop a high-level roadmap to inform the sponsoring executives. Then they start the requirements phase. After requirements are collected and analysed at a reasonable amount, the next important activity is to prioritise the requirements based on business impact.

Enterprise Architects need to develop criteria to prioritise the requirements based on factors depicted in the strategy and roadmap documents, as well as the financial and business priorities set by the sponsoring executives.

Applying a rigorous enterprise architecture approach is a critical aspect of modernisation initiatives. In addition to chairing Architecture Review Board, Enterprise Architects also perform the role of a Design Authority at the enterprise level. Enterprise Architects must have strategic, architectural thinking, and design thinking skills.

Enterprise Architects must understand the overall modernisation scope for enterprise, modernisation requirements, and use cases of the modernisation solutions.

Enterprise Architects must regularly assess risks, issues, dependencies and constraints considering strengths, weaknesses, opportunities and threats to support enterprise modernisation initiatives. To this end, they maintain a dynamic Viability Assessment work product at the enterprise level.

A dynamic and flexible governance model is essential for modernisation initiatives. The traditional stringent and extreme rule-based oppressive governance models can be roadblocks to the progress.

Enterprise Architects performing modernisation programs must have technical eminence and distinct technology expertise covering a broad spectrum of technologies, applications, data processing, and business processes in all IT domains.

Enterprise Architects need to communicate the business vision, strategy, plans, goals, and benefits of enterprise architecture efforts across all IT organisations and lines of business.

Enterprise Architects must articulate the most complex situations and technical matters to all stakeholders in a language that those people can understand by customising messages based on audience profile.

Enterprise Architects in modernisations initiatives must be innovators and innovation catalysts. They need to be creative and original thinkers. They need to provide architectural and technical mentorship to all stakeholders in the enterprise.

Enterprise Architects must be catalysts for ongoing change. With their catalytical contributions, they need to refresh the culture to more agile, collaborative, inventive, and innovative landscapes in the enterprise.

As active leaders and teachers, Enterprise Architects must create innovative learning opportunities for themselves and their team members. Enterprise Architects need to perform talent management and facilitation roles. They need to be very cautious to nurture and retain valuable talent in their teams.

Building high-performance teams are critical for the success of enterprise modernisation. Enterprise Architects must create collaborative, well-functioning, and high performing teams to run successful digital transformation initiatives.

Enterprise Architects need to articulate situations with constructive feedback, lots of clarifying examples, metaphors, and similes. This influential articulation focus can help people to see their blind spots, understand their weaknesses, and turn them into strengths.

In modernisation programs, Enterprise Architects need to use Key Performance Indicators. They must use team dashboards to see the trends and qualify and quantify progress in visual formats for the team members and the business stakeholders.

Thought leadership is a critical need and demand in modernisation environments, for changing cultures, and transforming ecosystems. Innovation starts with thinking differently. Innovative thinking requires multiple modes of thinking.

Enterprise Architects need to pay special attention to providing tangible outcomes with the support of their team members. The modernising environment presents a constant and rapid change and any change matters in the transforming ecosystem.

Some commonly used techniques for horizontal thinking are randomisations, distortions, reversals, exaggerations, metaphors, analogies, dreaming, theme mining, questioning the norms, and creating contradictions.

As innovation catalysts for modernisation, Enterprise Architect need to support the innovative culture and water the innovation garden regularly to survive and thrive.

To ignite innovation, Enterprise Architects must consider market conditions, client needs, and map them organisation's capabilities then define the focus areas for innovation agenda to enable digital transformation.

As customer-centric professionals, Enterprise Architects must lead to a mindset shift in small and large teams. They must hold a positive 'can do' attitude for any challenges they have.

Enterprise Architects must recognise those people who try to sabotage innovation in the modernisation programs. Even though these people with a negative mindset may be in the minority, they still can have a tremendous adverse impact on innovation in organisations.

Simplicity is a crucial pillar in our enterprise modernisation framework. Simplicity can empower enterprise modernisation. Simplicity is a substantial factor affecting digital transformations and modernisation programs.

Enterprise Architects need to articulate the most complicated and complex matters in a simple format that is understandable by others. However, simplicity requires in-depth knowledge and flexible thinking.

The best way of providing simplicity to the consumer is to think like the consumers. Enterprise Architects must keep focusing on the core tenets of simplifying products and services for the best possible user experience and satisfactory consumption merits.

Design simplicity has a tremendous impact on the subsequent phases of the modernisation lifecycle, such as service delivery and support. The simpler the design, the more effective the delivery and better service support can be.

Designing complex systems also require simplifications through modular and service-oriented designs. Modularity and modular approaches to complex solutions are essential for simplification, modernisation, and digital transformation. User stories are simple templates, including the functionalities, capabilities, and specifications from users or consumers point of view.

Refraining from convoluted phrases and instead, use of precise language and explicit statements are essential factors in simplifying communication. While Enterprise Architects can use advanced business terms to senior executives to articulate a point, they need to use deep technical terms to talk with engineers or technical specialists.

Simplicity in written communication is essential. People don't have much time and brainpower to understand intricate details in a technical document. The authors in enterprise modernisation initiatives must be sharp and to the point with clear statements. Short sentences are always preferable to improve readability.

Complex and complicated governance processes and procedures can be a hurdle for enterprise modernisation initiatives. The simplicity can be achieved through the right data analysis, intelligence, powerful tools, and effective management strategies. In other words, when correctly and purposefully analysed, more data can add better intelligence for modernising the data platforms.

Being brief and concise in presentations is also an essential simplification method for effective communication. For example, we can simplify team presentations by cutting unnecessary, irrelevant details and using a concise number of slides focusing on necessary points when using a PowerPoint as a tool.

Speed to market is one of the most fundamental requirements of businesses nowadays. Agile became the new norm in modernising enterprises. Products are expected to be released faster than they were in the past. Security updates and bug fixes are required more frequently.

There are many unknowns in the enterprise. Hence, it is not possible to see the end product without constant trial and error with structured experimentation in smaller scales to achieve modernisation goals.

An agile approach allows the team members to test their ideas iteratively. If they fail, they fail quickly and cheaply without costing lots of funds to the initiatives.

Enterprise Architects must develop mental models on how technology users interact with their solution in each iteration. With their action-oriented approach, they must use the backlogs quickly and in priority orders.

Enterprise Architects must take a pragmatic approach to architecture development when engaged in modernisation programs. We know that predicting the future is very hard; therefore, creating an upfront paragon of architecture is not practical.

Enterprise Architects need to understand the value of automation. Applying automation to modernisation goals, we can reduce the number of resources required to maintain manual and tedious systems. Automation can address human errors and resolve potential errors quickly.

Enterprise Architects continuously need to deal with culture and modernising ecosystem implications. They must strive to break silos, instead of coming above, they create flat structures, resulting in collaborative self-managing teams with many domain experts as peers.

Even though it is called 'fail fast' it refers to constant trial and error leading to further intelligence and learning to deal with unknowns in a fast and effective way. Learnings from these trial and errors constitute the progress for designing, developing and implementing complex solutions for enterprise modernisation goals.

Agile Enterprise Architects responsible for enterprise modernisation initiatives are capable of turning costs to investment. With a strong vision, innovative approaches, and agile delivery capabilities, the costs incurred from the initiatives of these architects can be seen as an investment.

Collaboration is an essential factor for Enterprise Architects to create outstanding results. These architects collaborate widely and productively. They also motivate their team members to collaborate effectively and efficiently by pointing out the common goals and making them compelling for collaboration.

The notion of fusion relates to concepts such as integration, blending, merging, amalgamation, and bonding. Fusion is closely related to collaboration from several angles. It is a type of collaboration designed for specific and advanced missions. Fusion principles suit the goals of enterprise modernisation.

Effective communication is a critical enabler of collaboration. Depending on the medium, both verbal and written communication types are essential for collaboration to happen. By focusing on productive collaboration at various levels, Enterprise Architects leverage insights from cross-functional teams and community of practices to create differentiated value propositions for the modernisation goals.

This magical aspect of collaboration leading to innovation is an ideal situation for modernisation goals.

Enterprise Architects must take advantage of this desirable situation by creating, maintaining, facilitating and further improving the situations.

Credibility in technical environments is critical. Enterprise Architects must be credible. These architects can earn the trust of their collaborators with credibility and integrity. Strategic Enterprise Architects must pay special attention to remain credible in their fields.

Trust is a requirement for diversity. Only with trust and trusted environments, people can show their true identities. When people start showing their true self, a diverse culture starts flourishing. Diversity is an enhancer of collaboration.

The key technology enablers of enterprise modernisation are Cloud Computing, Mobile Technologies, IoT, Big Data, and Analytics. An integrated view of these technologies, associated processes and tools are critical. Besides, benchmarking of products and services are essential enablers of digital transformations. We can use Cloud as a foundational enterprise modernisation tool. The cloud service model can expand or reduce computer resources based on service requirements.

The bottom line is that IoT is valuable for both business and economy, which is inevitable. From our current experience, we can construe that IoT will most likely have a substantial impact on our economy and the way we do business and commerce. IoT is an empowering enabler for enterprise modernisation.

Even though architecturally similar to traditional data, big data requires newer methods and tools to deal with data. Big Data analytics is a broad and growing area. We can better understand Big data analytics looking at its inherent characteristics.

Machine learning refers to computer systems to learn and improve based on their learning from the analysis of large volumes of data sets without programming. It is part of the artificial intelligence domain in computer science. Due to its usefulness and impact, machine learning became a vital technology and tool for enterprise modernisation strategies leading to digital transformation.

Text analytics include computational linguistics, machine learning, and traditional statistical analysis. Text analytics focus on converting massive volumes of a machine or human-generated text into meaningful structures to create business insights and support decision-making.

Cybersecurity is a necessary skill for Enterprise Architects working on modernisation initiatives. Cloud Computing, IoT and Big Data also mandate security at all levels. Broader security awareness and associated skills are essential for technical and technology leaders leading the modernisation and digital transformation initiatives.

Since the network and associated communication technologies are the fundamental enablers of enterprise modernisation goals, understanding functions of network and network implications such as security, latency, bandwidth, are also important topics that technology leaders need to cover broadly and in-depth based on their involvement.

Mobility is a critical interrelated technology domain in organisations hence Enterprise Architects need to understand and educate their teams for the effective use of mobility for innovations leading to business insights and collaboration across the organisation including the customers and partners.

IT service management covers an extensive array of technology, process, and tools. IT service management includes processes such as change management, problem management, incident management, service level management, capacity management, availability management, business continuity management, security management.

Cloud is a critical technology and service model for modern enterprises and workplaces. This technology is part of many modernisation and transformation programs globally.

The cloud service model can be a perfect fit to empower enterprise modernisation and transformation initiatives. The most desirable attributes of Cloud Computing are elasticity and scalability.

Pay-per-use and on-demand are other characteristics of the Cloud services model. Consumers can use when they demand the required services without upfront payment or dedicated investment for the IT resources in their organisation.

Flexible workload movement is another crucial attribute of Cloud service model. There may be times an organisation requires to run their workloads in a different time zone. In this case, we can quickly move the workloads to a data centre in another region or country.

Cloud services offer three primary service models. The popular models are IaaS (Infrastructure as a Service), PaaS (Platform as a Service) and SaaS (Software as a Service). There are also several other service types, but instead of using their names, we collectively call them XaaS.

Another fundamental point that we need to know is the deployment model for Cloud. There are four types of deployment models for Cloud-based services. They are public, private, hybrid, and community.

After Private and Public, the third model is the Hybrid Cloud, which is an integrated combination of Private and Public Offerings. For example, an organisation can use Private Cloud for their particular workload, which may require security and regulatory compliance.

Cost is the number one factor in enterprise modernisation initiatives. To deal with this critical factor, Enterprise Architects need to develop smart cost models for creating Cloud roadmaps. A simple cost model can include a comparison of building your own Cloud versus subscribing to a Cloud service provider.

There may be many hidden costs both in building your own Cloud or subscribing to Public Cloud services. Some hidden costs that we identified during some assessments were the cost of patch management, system tuning, ongoing training, end-user device support, hardware and software refresh. Optimisation of many components such as compute power, storage, network, facilities, middleware, applications, and data is critical.

Once we categorise the workloads in the architectural and planning phase, we can make decisions on which workload to deploy in which Cloud service models. Then, these decisions go to the design and deployment phases in the enterprise modernisation lifecycle.

Cloud, Big Data and IoT are the foremost enablers of enterprise modernisation initiatives nowadays. IoT, Big Data and Cloud Computing are three distinct technology domains with overlapping use cases.

Business continuity and disaster recovery must be implemented, tested and validated. We need to check whether the cloud services we consider are independently audited.

System integration facilities, APIs also need to be made available in the Cloud hosting services. We need to check whether we can integrate our solutions based on available integration infrastructure and tools.

To start the Cloud adoption process for our Big Data solutions in modernisation programs, we need to create a comprehensive Cloud transition plan. This plan must cover every aspect of the adoption with multiple stakeholders in the organisation.

One significant fact is that Big Data is ubiquitous in enterprises. Every enterprise generates massive amounts of data. Big data is different from traditional data. The main differences come from characteristics such as volume, velocity, variety, veracity, value and overall complexity of data sets in a data ecosystem.

The descriptive analytics deals with situations such as what is happening right now based on incoming data. The predictive analytics refers to what might happen in the future. Prescriptive analytics deals with actions to be taken. Diagnostic analytics ask the question of why something happened. Each analytics type serves difference scenarios and use-cases.

We can classify the process under two broad categories. The first one is Data Management, and the second one is Data Analytics. We need to understand data management activities such as data acquisition, extraction, cleansing, annotation, processing, integration, aggregation, and representation. Data Analytics components at a high level are activities such as modelling, analysis, interpretation, and visualisation.

Data governance is a critical factor for Big Data solutions. The Big Data governance system needs to consider essential factors such as security, privacy, trust, operability, conformance, agility, innovation and transformation of data.

Big Data governance is a broad area and covers components, scope, requirements handling, strategy, architecture, design, development, analysis, tests, processing, components, relationships, input, output, business goals, insights, and all other aspects of data management and analytics. Enterprise Architects are responsible for end to end governance of Big Data architecture and the associated solutions.

Most of the methods are proprietary; however, some are available via open-source programs. Some popular tools frequently mentioned in the Big Data Analytics publications are Aqua Data Studio, Azure HDinsight, IBM SPSS Modeler, Skytree, Talend, Splice Machine, Plotly, Lumify, Elasticsearch.

Some commonly used open-source analytics tools are Apache Hadoop, Apache Spark, Apache Storm, Apache Cassandra, Apache SAMOA, Neo4j, MongoDB, and R programming environment.

Enterprise Architects also need to understand various methods and techniques used for Big Data Analytics. Most commonly used methods and techniques for Big Data Analytics are natural language processing, two-sample hypothesis testing, machine learning, data mining, association pattern mining, behavioural analytics, predictive analytics, descriptive analytics, prescriptive analytics, diagnostic analytics.

Big Data architecture solutions require the use of the data lake model at the enterprise level. Data lakes are fundamental and useful aspects of Big Data lifecycle management. A data lake can be a single store of transformed enterprise data in the native format. The business value of data lakes come from being able to perform advanced analytics very quickly for data coming from various real-time sources such as clickstreams, social media, system logs.

Big Data solutions require heterogeneous technology and tools to fit the purpose. It is essential to realise that there is no single technology or tool which can provide all-purpose for developing Big Data solutions.

Modularity is another architectural consideration for Big Data solutions for enterprise modernisation goals. For modularity, we need to ensure the modules fits into the big picture. For example, the same data should be able to be used by different projects and technologies rather than creating unnecessary data access silos.

ACID (Atomicity, Consistency, Isolation, Durability) compliance is an essential guide to guarantee the validity of database transactions and sequence of operations when internal errors or system failures occur.

CAP (Consistency, Availability, and Partition) is another architectural point to consider for distributed database systems. This proposition instructs that a trade-off must be made choosing one out of three.

We need to choose the type of processing to perform whether real-time or batch processing. Our data processing may involve descriptive, predictive, prescriptive, diagnostic, and ad-hoc.

Data access patterns are necessary to optimise data access requirements. There are many patterns available in data application integration and interface publications. For example, some common patterns are accelerating database resource initialisation, eliminating data access bottlenecks, and hiding obscure database semantics from data users.

There are many open-source tools and technologies for Big Data and Analytics, such as Hadoop, Kafka, Flume, Sqoop, and Cassandra. An awareness of these tools is fundamental for Enterprise Architects.

Some of the most popular Big Data and Analytics platforms with associated tools are Google BigQuery, Hortonworks Data Platform, HP Bigdata, IBM Big Data, Microsoft Azure, SAP Bigdata Analytics, Teradata Bigdata Analytics, Amazon Web Services.

The main benefit and value proposition of IoT comes from collecting an enormous amount of data from various means and devices in the enterprise and then building services based on analyses of these massive amounts of data.

As IoT synthesises data via cognitive analytics, IoT solutions can help us gain better insights from structured, semi-structured, unstructured, dynamic or static data by integrating with cognitive systems.

From an architectural perspective, we need to be aware that IoT devices generate massive amounts of data on an ongoing basis. These data sets go to the full data management life cycle; for example, in storing, analysing, re-building, and archiving.

Due to potential implications for enterprise, we must plan data collection via IoT sensors carefully. First, we need to determine the type of physical signals to measure. Then, we need to identify the number of sensors to be used and the speed of signals for these sensors in our data acquisition plan.

Using benchmarks for application, data, and infrastructure, we need to create an exclusive IoT performance model and a set of test strategies for modernisation solutions.

We must be mindful that the monitoring of these devices also creates a tremendous amount of data. If we always add the alerts and other system management functions to keep these devices well-performing and available, we need to have a comprehensive performance model.

One of the business value propositions of IoT for enterprise modernisation is the integration of Cloud to IoT, which can create new revenue streams for the organisation.

Another architectural consideration for IoT is the use of Edge computing. When integrated with Edge computing, Cloud computing can add better value to the IoT ecosystem. The main reason for this is that Edge computing can do the filtering for the Cloud to focus on the usable data.

Enterprise Architects also need to focus on the representation of data available to enterprise consumers in visually compelling formats.

IoT Solutions require overall scalability and capacity plans. IoT applications integrate with and serve multiple devices in the ecosystem.

Maintaining the interoperability in an IoT ecosystem is another challenge owing to the wealth of platforms, solution components, devices and protocols used in IoT ecosystems.

Network bottlenecks adversely affect availability, performance and the cost of products or services in productions, making the service level agreements challenging to meet.

Several considerations also need to be made when it comes to internet connectivity; for example, the type of Internet services, internet service providers, usage cost, communication speed.

The major IoT concerns revolve around security and privacy for the enterprise. Privacy is related to security. It is well-known that security risks can cause privacy issues. IoT privacy concerns are complex and complicated due to their nature.

Enterprise mobility is a critical aspect of modernisation. Mobility involves people, process, technology and tools at a massive scale. Lifecycle management for mobile devices is an essential architectural consideration in enterprise modernisation initiatives. Managing mobile devices can be daunting from many angles.

In addition to quantity, the user in the enterprise may change the mobile devices frequently. These frequent changes require consideration of applications and software updates for these devices.

The security implications of mobile devices are massive challenges. They create many security vulnerabilities for enterprises. Software updates can be persistent and very frequent.

Mobile business intelligence, also known as Mobile BI is an essential requirement for enterprises to stay competitive, open new markets, and create new revenue streams. Some established and popular Mobile BI environments are publicly accessible services such as Appstore by Apple, Google Play Store, and Samsung Galaxy Store.

Enterprise modernisation programs can model these well-functioning services to create and improve their current Mobile BI strategy, service models, and offerings.

With this summary, we reached the end of this book. I authored this book to provide valuable guidance, compelling ideas, and unique ways to Enterprise Architects so that they can successfully perform complex enterprise modernisation initiatives transforming from chaos to coherence. This is not an ordinary theory book describing Enterprise Architecture in detail.

As a practising Enterprise Architect, I read many books and articles to learn different views from various enterprise architecture publications. They have been valuable to me to establish my foundations in the earlier phase of my profession. I attempted to author this book because I did not come across a concise guidance book showing Enterprise Architects the novel approaches, insights from the real-life experience and experimentations, and pointing out the differentiating technologies for enterprise modernisation.

The biggest lesson learned from my experience was the business outcome of the enterprise modernisation. What genuinely matters for business is the return on investment of the enterprise architecture and its monetising capabilities. The rest is the theory because nowadays sponsoring executives, due to economic climate, have no interest, attention, or tolerance for non-profitable ventures. I might have disappointed some idealistic Enterprise Architects, but with due respect, this view reflects the reality, and we cannot change it. I deal with pragmatic reality rather than theoretical perfection.

I attempted to show significant pain points and valuable considerations for enterprise modernisation using a structured approach. I hope you found this book a concise, uncluttered, and easy-to-read.

I overemphasised the architectural rigour on purpose. We cannot compromise the rigour aiming to the quality of products and services as a target outcome for modernisation goals in the enterprise. However, there must be a delicate balance among architectural rigour, business value, and speed to market. I applied this pragmatic approach to multiple substantial transformation initiatives and complex modernisations programs. The key point is using an incrementally progressing iterative approach to every aspect of modernisation initiatives, including people, processes, tools, and technologies as a whole.

Starting with a high-level view of enterprise architecture to set the context, I provided a dozen of distinct chapters to point out and elaborate on the factors which can make a real difference in dealing with complexity and producing excellent modernisation initiatives.

As eminent leaders, [probably you are one of them as the reader of this book] Enterprise Architects are the critical talents who can undertake this massive mission using their people and technology skills, in addition to many critical attributes outlined in the book. We need to assert the notion that Enterprise Architects are architects, not firefighters. I have full confidence that this book provided valuable insights for these talented architects to tackle this enormous mission in the modernising enterprise turning chaos to coherence.

Appendix: Other Books by this Author

From an architectural perspective, the following books can be useful to further understand the technologies mentioned in this book.

Architecting Digital Transformation

12-step Architectural Leadership Method

Enterprises are facing enormous challenges to respond to the rapid changes and growing demands of digital consumers globally. There is constant search to find solutions to the growing problems. The most optimal solution to address this problem is to architect our enterprise digital transformation requirements aligning with digital trends and innovative frameworks as described in this book with an articulated 12-step method.

Architecting digital transformations address the root causes of fundamental issues that we experience in the digital world. The proliferation of digital media in the form of images, sound, and videos created a massive demand for our infrastructure to scale globally. Relentless sharing of these media types creates an unsustainable load over the networks, applications, and other expensive infrastructure components unless an effective capacity plan is in place.

Based on my architectural thought leadership on various enterprise architecture initiatives, digital transformation, and modernisation engagements, with my accumulated body of knowledge and skills from practical settings, I want to share these learnings in a concise book with a specific 12-step method hoping to add value by contributing to the broader digital community and the progressing digital transformation initiatives.

I made every effort to make this book concise, uncluttered, and easy-to-read by removing technical jargons to make it readable by a broader audience who want to architect their digital transformation programs to align with the growing demands of their digital consumers. In this book, I highlight the problems from an architectural point of view, following established and emerging methods, and recommend effective solutions to address them in a methodical way.

What distinguishes this book from other books on the market is that I provide a practical framework and a methodical approach to architect your organisation's digital infrastructure, applications, data, security, and other components based on experience, aiming not to sell or endorse any products or services to you.

A Practical Guide for IoT Solution Architects

Architecting secure, agile, economic, highly available, well-performing IoT ecosystems

The focus of this book is to provide IoT solution architects with practical guidance and a unique perspective. Solution architects working in IoT ecosystems have an unprecedented level of responsibility at work; therefore, dealing with IoT ecosystems can be daunting.

As an experienced practitioner of this topic, I understand the challenges faced by the IoT solution architects. In this book, I have reflected upon my insights based on my solution architecture experience spread across three decades. In addition, this book can also guide other architects and designers who want to learn the architectural aspects of IoT and understand the key challenges and practical resolutions in

IoT solution architectures. Each chapter focuses on the key aspects that form the framing scope for this book; namely, security, availability, performance, agility, and cost-effectiveness.

In this book, I have also provided useful definitions, a brief practical background on IoT and a guiding chapter on solution architecture development. The content is mainly practical; hence, it can be applied or be a supplemental input to the architectural projects at hand.

Architecting Big Data Solutions Integrated with IoT & Cloud

Create strategic business insights with agility

IoT, Big Data, and Cloud Computing are three distinct technology domains with overlapping use cases. Each technology has its own merits; however, the combination of three creates a synergy and the golden opportunity for businesses to reap the exponential benefits. This combination can create technological magic for innovation when adequately architected, designed, implemented, and operated.

Integrating Big Data with IoT and Cloud architectures provide substantial business benefits. It is like a perfect match. IoT collects real-time data. Big Data optimises data management solutions. Cloud collects, hosts, computes, stores, and disseminates data rapidly.

Based on these compelling business propositions, the primary purpose of this book is to provide practical guidance on creating Big Data solutions integrated with IoT and Cloud architectures. To this end, the book offers an architectural overview, solution practice, governance, and underlying technical approach for creating integrated Big Data, Cloud, and IoT solutions.

The book offers an introduction to solution architecture, three distinct chapters comprising Big Data, Cloud, and the IoT with the final chapter, including conclusive remarks to consider for Big Data solutions. These chapters include essential architectural points, solution practice, methodical rigour, techniques, technologies, and tools.

Creating Big Data solutions are complex and complicated from multiple angles. However, with the awareness and guidance provided in this book, the Big Data solutions architects can be empowered to provide useful and productive solutions with growing confidence.

A Technical Excellence Framework for Innovative Digital Transformation Leadership

Transform enterprise with technical excellence, innovation, simplicity, agility, fusion, and collaboration

The primary purpose of this book is to provide valuable insights for digital transformational leadership empowered by technical excellence by using a pragmatic five-pillar framework. This empowering framework aims to help the reader understand the common characteristics of technical and technology leaders in a structured way.

Even though there are different types of leaders in broad-spectrum engaging in digital transformations, in this book, we only concentrate on excellent technical and technology leaders having digital transformation goals to deal with technological disruptions and robust capabilities to create new revenue streams. No matter whether these leaders may hold formal executive titles or just domain specialist titles, they demonstrate vital characteristics of excellent technical leadership capabilities enabling them to lead complex and complicated digital transformation initiatives.

The primary reason we need to understand technical excellence and required capabilities for digital transformational leadership in a structured context is to model their attributes and transfer the well-known characteristics to the aspiring leaders and the next generations. We can transfer our understanding of these capabilities at an individual level and apply them to our day to day activities. We can even turn them into useful habits to excel in our professional goals. Alternatively, we can pass this information to other people that we are responsible for, such as our teenagers aiming for digital leadership roles, tertiary students, mentees, and colleagues.

We attempt to define the roles of strategic technical and technology leaders using a specific framework, based on innovation, simplicity, agility, collaboration, fusion and technical excellence. This framework offers a common understanding of the critical factors of the leader. The structured analysis presented in this book can be valuable to understand the contribution of technical leaders clearly.

Admittedly, this book has a bias towards the positive attributes of excellent leaders on purpose. The compelling reason for this bias is to focus on the positive aspects and describe these attributes concisely in an adequate amount to grasp the topic so that these positive attributes can be reused and modelled by the aspiring leaders. As the other side of the coin is also essential for different insights, I plan to deal with the detrimental aspects of useless leaders in a separate book, perhaps under the lessons learned context considering different use cases for a different audience type. Consequently, I excluded the negative aspects of useless leaders in this book.

Digital Intelligence

I authored this book because dealing with intelligence, and the digital world is a passion for me and wanted to share my passion with you. In this book, I aim to provide compelling ideas and unique ways to increase, enhance, and deepen your digital intelligence and awareness and apply them to your organisation's digital journey particularly for modernisation and transformation initiatives. I used the architectural thinking approach as the primary framework to convey my message.

Based on my architectural thought leadership on various digital transformation and modernisation engagements, with the accumulated wealth of knowledge and skills, I want to share these learnings in a concise book hoping to add value by contributing to the broader digital community and the progressing initiatives.

Rest assured, this is not a theory or an academic book. It is purely practical and based on lessons learned from real enterprise transformation and modernisation initiatives taken in large corporate environments.

I made every effort to make this book concise, uncluttered, and easy-to-read by removing technical jargons for a broader audience who want to enhance digital intelligence and awareness.

Upfront, this book is not about a tool, application, a single product, specific technology, or service, and certainly not to endorse any of these items. However, this book focuses on architectural thinking and methodical approach to improve digital intelligence and awareness. It is not like typical digital transformation books available on the market. In this book, I do not cover and repeat the same content of those books describing digital transformations.

My purpose is different. What distinguishes this book

from other books is that I provide an innovative thinking framework and a methodical approach to increase your digital quotient based on experience, aiming not to sell or endorse any products or services even though I mention some prominent technologies which enable digital transformation, for your digital awareness, intelligence, and capabilities.

About the Author

Dr Mehmet Yildiz is a Distinguished Enterprise Architect L3 certified from the Open Group. Working in the IT industry over the last 35 years leading complex enterprise projects for large corporate organisations, he focuses on cutting edge technology solutions, such as IoT, Big Data Analytics, Blockchain, Cognitive, AI, Cloud, Fog, and Edge Computing integration.

Mehmet is a hands-on enterprise practitioner for solution architectures leading complex enterprise initiatives and a selected Agile champion for his pragmatic delivery. As an innovation evangelist in all walks of his life, he is also a recognised inventor with several patents.

For his professional giveback activities, Mehmet generously shares his expertise, teaches the best architectural and design practices at work, mentors his colleagues, supervises doctoral students and provides industry-level lectures to postgraduate students at several universities in Australia.

As a prolific writer, Mehmet reflects the insights from his real work field to provide value to his readers using a personalised and plain narration. His content is original, simplified, and aims to address the compelling issues of the digital world and modern corporate enterprises. He notably refrains from theoretical and convoluted content in his books.

LinkedIn. https://www.linkedin.com/in/mehmetyildiz

Goodreads: https://www.goodreads.com/drmehmetyildiz

Publications: https://digitalmehmet.com

www.ingramcontent.com/pod-product-compliance
Lightning Source LLC
Chambersburg PA
CBHW051052050326
40690CB00006B/698